Pre-school Parenting Secrets

Talking
with the Sky

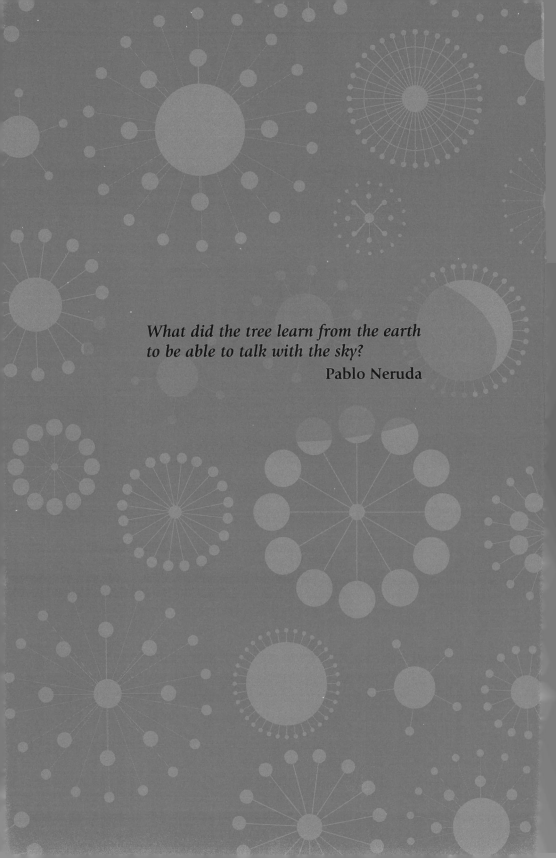

*What did the tree learn from the earth
to be able to talk with the sky?*

Pablo Neruda

Foreword by coauthor of *Einstein Never Used Flash Cards*

Pre-school Parenting Secrets

Talking with the Sky

Learn What Over 10,000 Hours of Research Show
About Your Pre-school Child

by
Brian Caswell and David Chiem

in collaboration with
Kylie Bell

World Scientific

NEW JERSEY · LONDON · SINGAPORE · BEIJING · SHANGHAI · HONG KONG · TAIPEI · CHENNAI

Published by

World Scientific Publishing Co. Pte. Ltd.

5 Toh Tuck Link, Singapore 596224

USA office: 27 Warren Street, Suite 401-402, Hackensack, NJ 07601

UK office: 57 Shelton Street, Covent Garden, London WC2H 9HE

Library of Congress Cataloging-in-Publication Data
Caswell, Brian
  Pre-school parenting secrets: Talking with the sky / Brian Caswell,
  David Chiem & Kylie Bell.
    p. cm.
  Includes bibliographical references.
  ISBN-13: 978-981-4317-09-2
  ISBN-10: 981-4317-09-8
  1. Child rearing. 2. Parenting. 3. Parent and child. I. Chiem, David. II. Bell, Kylie.
  III. Title.
  HQ767.9.C438 2010
  649'.123--dc22
                                                            2010020452

British Library Cataloguing-in-Publication Data
A catalogue record for this book is available from the British Library.

In-house Editor: Juliet Lee Ley Chin

Printed in Singapore by Mainland Press Pte Ltd.

The Physical, Emotional and Social Needs of Your Pre-school Child

FOREWORD

What is the world our children will face 25 years from now when they enter the workforce? How different will that world be from the rapidly evolving world we face today? By all accounts, people will move from job to job as independent 'e-lancers', sticking to one job about as long as their loyalty to a brand of toothpaste. Many will work from home as the trend away from centralised offices continues. This calls for a different kind of education. This future calls for an education that emphasises thinking on one's feet, flexibility and creative thinking.

The educational establishment of today is not equipped to provide children with the skills they need. Until that establishment slowly crawls in the right direction and morphs into the butterfly we need, today's parents should understand how the world their children will face demands a different kind of experience than the one we had as children. Where can parents find the secrets of raising children with the qualities they will need for success?

Go to any random page in *Pre-school Parenting Secrets: Talking with the Sky* and you will find these nuggets. Take this quotation on creativity:

In an ideal 21st Century curriculum, the quality and creativeness of a child's thought processes are seen as a more highly valued outcome of education than the mere acquisition of given information.

The authors are so right. With information doubling every 2.5 years, the last thing we need our children to do is slavishly memorise content that will be outmoded before they can use it. This is not to say that memorisation by itself is bad; indeed, children need to learn the strategies required to a) select the most important information; and b) commit it to memory. But we are no longer talking about just *retrieval* of information; what is needed for tomorrow is the ability to retrieve and then transform. Our children will be judged on their ability to combine information in new ways to solve problems that haven't yet emerged.

Pre-school Parenting Secrets: Talking with the Sky is a parent's guide to providing children with the skills they will need for the future. It is a delightful compendium of ideas and practices and social strategies that can help children reach their fullest potential. Written in a delightful and highly approachable style, this volume can help any parent do a better job in raising well-adjusted, happy and intelligent children.

What David Chiem, Brian Caswell and Kylie Bell appreciate is that *brains* are not enough. Brains only get children ahead when they are embedded in a social body that understands itself and others. Brains only matter when they can do more than 'spit back' information unchanged — when they can communicate ideas effectively.

In our 2009 book *A Mandate for Playful Learning in Preschool* we touted the 6Cs[TMI] — **Collaboration** (the ability to work with others), **Communication** (the ability to transmit one's ideas orally or in writing; to be persuasive), **Content** (mastery of the subjects taught in school, including the arts), **Creative Innovation** (the ability to go beyond what is known), **Critical Thinking** (culling from among the vast amounts of information now available to us, to find the kernels we need), and **Confidence** (not stopping in the face of failure) as the skills children need for a 21st Century world. *Pre-school Parenting Secrets: Talking with the Sky* addresses the 6Cs[TM] without calling them by this name. It invites parents to see how children can develop these skills naturally and without tutors or special classes.

Parenting styles that take a child's perspective into consideration will always be more effective than those that impose adult thinking on the child before the child is ready to comprehend. As the authors write:

> **In order to make and maintain relationships, solve problems and resolve conflicts successfully, humans need to develop the ability to see the world from others' perspectives.**

But they don't just stipulate. This book provides numerous examples, explanations and activities that parents can use to help children develop the capacity to see 'others' perspectives'.

Parents who use this book will find their lives made infinitely easier, as their children's sometimes inexplicable behaviour is explained to them. Further, parents are offered insights, games and tactics that are generalisable and go beyond the specific situation in which they are showcased. In short, the best way to conclude this endorsement of a book I thoroughly enjoyed is to quote its authors on the subject of parenting:

> **Our role as parents is not to teach, but to facilitate. Our responsibility is not to control, but to assist — to provide the flexible structures within which our children can be creative and develop their unique understanding of the world and their place in it.**
>
> **Roberta M. Golinkoff**
> Wilmington DE, USA

❦

Roberta Golinkoff is the H. Rodney Sharp Professor in the School of Education and Departments of Psychology and Linguistics, and Cognitive Science at the University of Delaware. She is the co-author of: *Einstein Never Used Flash Cards: How Our Children Really Learn and Why They Should Play More and Memorize Less* (Rodale) and *A Mandate for Playful Learning in Preschool: Presenting the Evidence* (Oxford).

Roberta is also a recipient of the coveted **American Psychological Association's Distinguished Service Award** for her dissemination of information on educational research.

PREFACE

PLAY OR ENRICHMENT?
A PERFECTLY REASONABLE QUESTION

Which is more important — play or enrichment?

We run Parenting Strategies Workshops for thousands of people in a number of countries, and in one recent session, this question came up. It is a common theme among parents of this generation of pre-schoolers.

The young mother raising this particular issue was there to learn everything she could about providing her children (a lively four-year-old girl and a boy of maybe two or three) with whatever might be required to make them both happy and successful.

> **Sweet flowers are slow and weeds make haste.**
> **William Shakespeare**

She was clearly a caring and attentive parent, and it was a perfectly reasonable question, under the circumstances. Like parents in many wealthy countries, she wanted only the best that money could buy for her children — clothes, toys, nutrition...

Preparation for life...

That being said, it is a question which bears closer examination. Because it is a question that few parents might have asked — even as recently as a generation ago.

We have reached an interesting (and disturbing) tipping-point in our society, when we can even contemplate choosing between "play *or* enrichment".

> **For young children, play is enrichment. Play is how a child learns to make sense of the world, to mould together the tiny particles of experience that will lay the foundations of future creativity and intellectual development.**

Unfortunately, our society, both within its learning institutions, and outside them, has become dangerously — and quite unnecessarily — obsessed with forcing children to 'perform' and compete at younger and younger ages.

Life for a child in today's world is becoming more and more demanding. With strict criteria for entry into the 'best' kindergartens and primary schools (and sometimes, even pre-schools), most parents are looking for a way to give their child 'the competitive edge'.

This has led to the explosive growth of an 'enrichment' industry — replete with flash-cards, pseudo-scientific mumbo-jumbo about 'right- and left-brain (or even 'middle-brain') training' and 'critical windows of opportunity', DNA 'testing' or finger-print analysis to predict 'innate talents' — and children being ferried from one enrichment activity to the next with a frequency which would make an adult's head spin.

But these are not adults — nor even 'young adults'. They are children, and we are in grave danger of damaging their future development as successful human beings, by denying them their right to a childhood.

Ambitious parents point proudly to the number of enrichment activities to which they subject their children, without ever asking some very basic questions:

1 *Is all this stressful activity really necessary?*
2 *Is it actually benefitting my child?*
3 *Is my child enjoying the experience?*
4 *What is my real motivation for imposing this amount of pressure onto my child?*

If my motive is to impress other parents with my dedication to 'enriching' my child's experience, then it is time for a radical rethink.

Children are not status symbols. If you want to impress your neighbours, buy yourself a shiny red sports car.

This is not to say that we can't seek out ways to enrich our children's lives with new experiences — or even that we shouldn't introduce them to professionals who understand their needs and can help their developing minds to grow with enthusiasm. It is simply that in choosing that help, we must be alert for the exploitive, the naive, and, above all, the 'fashionable'.

As parents, we are the earth from which our children grow. How we prepare and fertilise the soil will define their relationship with the world. It will determine the nature of their lifelong conversation with the universe.

Time to Be a Child

If 'enrichment experiences' are not the key to producing a child who is 'all he or she can be', then what *is* the secret?

How *should* I bring up my children? What kind of experiences *do* I need to give them in their preschool years, so that I feel confident I have provided them with the best possible childhood?

The key, above all other things, is to give the child time. Time to bond. Time to be a child. Time to explore the world through play.

If my motive is to give my child an enjoyable and enriching experience (as opposed to a fashionable 'enrichment experience'), then perhaps the simple answer lies in learning what we can do — together — to broaden our mutual horizons, while strengthening the all-important parent-child bond.

Reading together, playing board games and puzzles, engaging in sports, making up shared stories, rolling on the floor or on the beach, having fun with numbers, words, colours and shapes...

These and a thousand other activities are all playful diversions which enrich a child's experience of the world. They encourage intellectual and emotional maturity in a natural and satisfying way — and they don't cost a thing.

More formal enrichment activities should always grow from the child's interests and needs. Do they show an interest in music? Art? Are they happiest when they are doing somersaults and cartwheels? What activities do they gravitate to by choice?

Science — or Pseudoscience?

Beware of false prophets, who promise the world, and try to blind you with 'pseudo-science'.

In the world of medicine, no drug or medical procedure can be sold or offered until it has been tested and researched thoroughly and its effects are a matter of public record.

There is no such regulation in the enrichment or education industries. This means that the unscrupulous — or the naively well-intentioned – can make any sort of untested claim with impunity.

Be particularly cautious if a programme or organisation:

i) **Claims 'miracle' results through some new and previously unknown discovery about the human brain.** Neuroscience is a science in its infancy, and the claims made about the 'powers' of the right-brain, or the ability to 'unlock genius' — or any specific talent — are simply not based on any reputable science. True geniuses are born — not made — and no reputable scientist would even claim to know what causes genius.

ii) **Bases its claims on the work of one 'guru' — especially if you search the web for his/her work, and the only references are on that organisation's own website.** The work of reputable scientists is always peer-reviewed — but generally, these 'gurus' are anything but reputable. Many are not even qualified in the science in which they claim to have made their 'breakthough'.

iii) **Is tied to the name of a 'motivational speaker' — who also, in other forums, offers advice on how to manipulate the stock market or other such adult-oriented 'skills'.** What may work to motivate adults, especially when the ethics are questionable anyway, has little to do with developing the minds of pre-schoolers — but many of these 'entrepreneurs' see parents as just another lucrative and easy 'market'.

Building on our children's passions is the surest way to enrich their experience. Observe your child and you will be guided towards the most appropriate (enjoyable) activities — which are the only ones that will be of any real benefit.

A Word of Caution

Always keep a check on whether it is your child's passion, or your own passion, unrealised, driving the activity. Know the difference between the children doing the activity for their own enjoyment, and doing it to please you — which they will most certainly do.

Research shows that if children do not enjoy an activity for its own sake, then they are likely to derive no lasting value from it.

> **The only truly effective way to home in on the passions that drive your children is to give them the widest possible range of day-to-day experiences — in an informal, unstructured way — so that they can discover for themselves what truly excites them.**

Of course, many parents live impossibly busy lives and, though they do their best, it is unrealistic to expect them to be able to drop everything and 'just play'. At least, not as often as is desirable.

What busy parents *can* do, however, is create the kind of home environment that is enriching for their child. This includes not just physical surroundings, but also the social/emotional climate. In the end, it is the home environment that has the greatest impact on early childhood development, not a series of 'enrichment' classes.

Many parents are anxious that by the time their children start school they not only have the minimum set of pre-academic skills — such as letter and number recognition — but that they are in fact 'advanced'. As if education is a race and a 'head start' will keep their child always at the front of the pack.

Unfortunately, learning does not work like this. The learning journey is rarely, if ever, straightforward. There are always challenges to overcome, crises to navigate and times which may see your child thrive or falter.

Ultimately, what is more important than loading children with basic demonstrable skills (like the alphabet and numbers) is the solid preparation of the internal framework they carry with them. It is this framework that makes them ready to learn, want to learn — love to learn — throughout their life.

> **Enriching a child's life means allowing that child to discover, through hands-on experience, how things work, and how to make them work better.**
>
> **By far the best way for a child to do that is through play — both structured and unstructured.**

There are many things parents can do in the crucial pre-school years that prepare their children to be fascinated, enthusiastic learners with a strong intellectual and emotional foundation from which to tackle any learning challenge. As you read on, you will learn to master many of these.

In 1998, we founded an organisation (called MindChamps) with the aim of providing young people with the help that every parent desires for every child.

As well as training parents in how to create a truly enriching home environment, we have, over the years, developed a unique pre-school curriculum, which nurtures all the key foundations of learning through games, guided imagination, music, movement and social interaction — with no drilling or 'flash-cards' in sight.

When developing out-of-school programmes for young children, we have always focussed on creating the fun, experiential, active and 'hands-on' foundation activities that children enjoy. This is the child-centred 'structured play' which experts around the world now recommend as the only truly effective path to productive lifelong learning. That is our definition of enrichment and in that, we are not alone.

The Oxford Dictionary defines enrichment as '*to make richer in quality, flavour etc.'.* True enrichment is not 'product oriented', and the Oxford definition mentions nothing about learning five languages by the age of five or becoming the next baby Mozart.

Pre-school Parenting Secrets: Talking with the Sky is the first volume of a two-volume series for the parents (and carers) of pre-school, kindergarten and early primary-aged children. It is not written as an academic text, and though we will, at times, discuss the science and the philosophy behind a strategy or an approach, we have kept the scientific details and philosophical discussion to a bare minimum.

For parents interested in following up on some of the ideas raised, we have included at the end of each volume a bibliography of some useful and enlightening books, web-pages and articles for you to read. *Pre-school Parenting Secrets: Talking with the Sky* is the result of more than 10,000 hours of research, hundreds of hands-on programmes, lectures and discussion sessions, and years of working closely with young people and their parents.

You have embarked upon an exciting journey — but any journey is easier with a roadmap. We hope that this book and its companion volume ***Pre-school Parenting Secrets: Wider than the Sky*** provide that roadmap, and help you to share more confidently in the excitement of the journey — from the crib to the classroom.

And beyond...

> **Our aim is to empower parents, with simple strategies (and lots of fun activities!) for creating healthy thoughts, feelings and attitudes within their children.**
>
> **Like thousands of parents across the world, you too can learn to nurture simple skills and behaviours in your child, to provide the foundations for a lifelong love of learning — for its own sake.**

CONTENTS

SERIES INTRODUCTION
The Seed in the Palm of Your Hand

CHAPTER ONE
The Science: What Research Tells Us About the Needs of a Child

SACHA

CHAPTER TWO

The Physical Needs: Understanding Your Child's Basic Physical Needs — Healthy Development Through Sensible Decision-Making

CHAPTER THREE

The Emotional Needs: The Power of Mindset — Building a Healthy and Resilient Self-Image in Your Child

CHAPTER FOUR

The Social Needs: Fostering Effective Communication and Social Skills

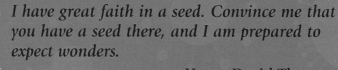

I have great faith in a seed. Convince me that you have a seed there, and I am prepared to expect wonders.

Henry David Thoreau

The Seed in the Palm of Your Hand

In our souls, we are all gardeners, whether we realise it or not.

We sow our seeds, and wait for them to sprout. We cultivate and water the seedlings, and we dream of the plants they will grow to be — and the fruits that they will bear.

In our souls, we are all gardeners, and our children are the plants we nurture.

But if you could hold in the palm of your hand any seed in the world, what kind of plant would you choose to sow?

1 The beautiful, but solitary rose, whose protective thorns ensure a lonely existence?

2 The fast-growing, but fragile hot-house flower that blooms early, then withers, unable to stand the heat or the cold?

3 A bonsai, special and unique, whose shape and dimensions reflect your desire for perfection — albeit limited by the size of the pot you place it in?

Or maybe, the Bamboo...

Consider the Bamboo — a Lesson in Preparation

The Bamboo is one of the most successful plants in the world, because much of its development happens beneath the ground, before new shoots even become visible.

> **The Bamboo has much to teach us about how we should — and shouldn't — approach the early years of our children's lives.**

A bamboo plant starts to spread by extending its roots and tendrils (called rhizomes) beneath the soil, colonising the surrounding area and giving itself extensive physical foundations and good access to the water and nutrition needed to sustain the mature plant.

Once all the required elements are in place, new shoots spring from the rhizomes and appear above the ground surface. They grow very quickly and strongly (some bamboo species grow up to 1.2 metres a day — or 5 centimetres per hour! — during their 'growth spurt') and the mature bamboo plant resists almost all natural threats in its environment — including typhoons — because it is flexible and because each element of its structure supports, and is supported by, every other element.

Compare the Bamboo with other plants we might choose to grow.

A Rose by Any Other Name...

Stand back and admire the rose, but don't get too close. Its petals are fragile and fall away at the slightest touch, and should you hold it to your breast you *will* feel its sting.

Many of today's children — even in their pre-school years — spend so much time in study and enrichment, 'refining their skills', preparing for success, searching for perfection, that there is little time for anything as 'unstructured' as play.

After all, if it can't be measured and graded, what use is it?

What *use*...?

> **It is in play that we learn who we are — who other people are — and how to 'get on' in a world in which 'inter-personal skills' are as vital as 'intelligence' and (more often than not) EQ trumps IQ in the employment market-place.**

The temptation, as a parent, is to try to help our children to avoid the 'pitfalls' of childhood — to control and modify their 'anti-social' behaviour — rather than creating a loose structure of rules, within which they can behave in a more unstructured way, and learn by trial and error what works and what doesn't.

If we try to control our children — their experiences and their environment — too rigidly when they are young, we squeeze out the playfulness, the messiness, of childhood.

Why is this dangerous?

Because we run the risk of reprimanding out of their lives the messy experimentation and silliness which teaches them what it means to be an interactive human being.

We might produce children who are well-presented and sit like perfectly-behaved 'Stepford children' when we go visiting — and even get praised for their beautiful manners.

Unfortunately, we also run the risk of stifling their personality growth — of creating teenagers and 'prickly' young adults who resist social interaction and whose identity is tied up in what they do (or how they appear) rather than who they are.

There is nothing wrong with imagining a beautiful rose, but why not imagine a superior rose — one without the thorns which isolate it from the world beyond itself?

Is there Life beyond the Hot-house?

We hear a great deal about 'hot-housing' our children, to give them the 'winning edge' in the 'competitive' world of early education. Perhaps we should be thinking more closely about the long-term effects of such a well-meaning but misguided policy.

Hot-house blooms can appear to develop quickly and attain maturity at an impressive rate, but as any gardener will tell you, they rarely make the transition to real-world conditions.

Of what use is it for a two-year-old to parrot the faces and names of famous artists — flashed before him on a set of five-by-four-inch cards — if he has no appreciation of the wonderful works those artists have produced? It may appear impressive, but it is no more miraculous than teaching a parrot to roller-skate. It can be done, and you can see the results on YouTube, but does the trick make the parrot a more effective bird? Of course not!

A bird is born to fly and soar. Why would you even *want* it to roller-skate?

Flash-card memorisation — one of the many useless strategies used to hot-house young children — does nothing more than cram the child's working memory with useless information. Where else in their lives will this 'trick' be of any use?

It is an unfortunate fact that the swift (and unnatural) development of hot-house flowers comes at a terrible price. They are not sufficiently prepared by their early, artificial development to cope with the demanding conditions they will inevitably meet beyond the walls of the hot-house, and they fail at the first sign of inclement weather.

In a rapidly-changing world, we can never predict the future environment to which our children, as adults, will need to respond. The traits of resilience and versatility are established in early childhood — through experience with the real world of trial and error.

So, unless you plan to keep your 'seedlings' trapped behind the glass of an unnatural environment for their entire existence, it's a good idea to avoid the hot-house completely.

The Bonsai — Art, or Arrested Development?

An Old English proverb states:

As the twig is bent, so grows the tree.

It is the same truth which underpinned the work of the bonsai artists of Ancient Japan — starting a tradition which has survived virtually unchanged down through the centuries to today.

A bonsai is, without doubt, a work of art and contemplation — a beautiful miniature; a reflection of perfection; nature confined to a pot, cut and trained and constantly manicured into the bonsai master's concept of what a tree should be.

A bonsai is Art imitating Life.

But is it the metaphor we want to follow, when it comes to our pre-schoolers?

Do we want to limit our children by pruning them and bending them to our will? Do we want stunted, compliant imitations or bold, creative thinkers — people who will conform, or people who will *reform*?

A tree that matures in the real world, adapts and responds to the climate, the weather and the soil — limited only by its own genetic imperatives.

If we concentrate too much on limiting the form — on restricting our vision of what could be, then we risk creating children who are 'pot-bound' for life.

Contrary to what some parents fervently believe, childhood is not about moulding a perfect mini adult. Early childhood is a stage of development in its own right. It is a training ground for future development. Micro-managing a child's development — especially in the early years — ignores the natural instincts and interests of the child, in favour of activities that the parent feels will create the perfect well-rounded adult.

Experience — messy and exciting and as unpredictable as real life — is what moulds a well-rounded adult, and you can't fit enough experience into one small pot to achieve that result!

> **The more we focus on 'force-feeding' our pre-school children to perform only in the artificial environment of a school — the more we design tasks whose only purpose is to compare and grade them at earlier and earlier ages — the less chance they will have to truly prepare for the life they will live in the demanding and changeable world of the 21ˢᵗ Century.**

Why the Bamboo?

In Asia, the Bamboo is a symbol of both longevity and friendship, and it is considered the most useful of all plants.

- Its shoots are edible, low calorie and nutritious.

- In architecture and construction, it is both ornamental and practical, being used as a hard, lightweight and exceptionally durable timber for buildings and furniture — even high-rise scaffolding and concrete reinforcing.

- In medicine, it has been widely employed to treat infection and respiratory diseases.

- Bamboo fibres are used to create a yarn which is woven into a soft, anti-bacterial fabric or to produce a kind of environmentally friendly paper.

- The list of its uses for household utensils, toys, musical instruments and furnishings — even skis and skateboards — is limited only by your imagination.

Which means that it is virtually limitless.

This wide versatility and resilience is, of course, an ideal metaphor for how we want all children to develop, but for the parents of younger children in particular, the lesson of the Bamboo is even more profound.

The foundation of its success is the system of roots that it develops before anything obvious happens above ground. To the casual observer, nothing much appears to be occurring, but the growth that is taking place out of sight is quite spectacular — and more importantly, it is the right sort of growth.

This is how it is with young children. When they play — when they experiment, hands-on, with all elements within their environment — connections are being made. They may not be able to explain them, they may not even be aware of them, but children's impressive creativity is evidence enough — if we care to pay attention — that important things are happening 'beneath the surface'.

As experiences accumulate, things begin to connect and make sense. Then children begin to understand, at a fundamental level, concepts which they will need in later life.

And understanding builds further connections. The 'root system' within their developing brains — the complex neural network upon which all future learning depends — is expanding and proliferating, preparing the ground for future growth.

The Power of 'Child's-Play'

It is often said that we live in a young person's world — that is, things are evolving so rapidly that only young people seem to be equipped to keep up with the changes. But this is an illusion.

As human beings, we are all capable of altering our understanding and our approach. What prevents us is a mindset — a way of looking at the world — which falls back on old habits and resists innovation.

We need to be open to innovation, to seeing things in a new way. If we are to keep up, we need to become more 'child-like'. We need to learn to play again, because play is the essence of innovation.

As George Bernard Shaw once wrote:

We don't stop playing because we grow old; we grow old because we stop playing.

Our children are experts at play, and as long as we don't 'organise it out of them', they will remain flexible and innovative. They will enjoy the challenge of an environment in flux. They will soar.

They will understand, as we need to understand, what Mark Twain recognised more than a century ago, when he said:

Work and play are words used to describe the same thing under differing conditions.

Or what creativity expert, Roger von Oech, so wisely pointed out, when he wrote:

Necessity may be the mother of invention, but play is certainly the father.

For more insight into the importance of play, look up the work of Dr Stuart Brown — the founder of the National Institute for PLAY. It will open your eyes to the Power of 'Child's-Play'. Also, look for books by Professors Kathy Hirsh-Pasek and Roberta Michnick Golinkoff whose work on early childhood learning is a revelation.

Children drilled and channelled into narrow, rigid, ways of behaving can certainly be trained to jump through the right hoops, even if they don't adequately understand what they are doing. After all, that's how we train dogs and lab rats — and children are far more intelligent than they are!

Without understanding, however, the learning isn't transferable — they can't apply it to anything except the particular (usually meaningless) task for which it was learned. The necessary wider connections are simply not being made.

Like the hot-house bloom or the bonsai, their neural 'root systems' are frail and limited, unable to support future growth.

Though such children may appear to shine at an early age, more often than not, it is a false dawn, which never quite lives up to its early promise.

Managing Change

The past half-century has produced the most profound social and intellectual changes in human history. Change will be the one constant in the lives of our children.

It is inescapable. Irresistible.

Manage change and you ride the leading edge of the wave as it carries you into the future. Resist it — or respond to it with fear — and it breaks over you, swamping your potential and drowning your dreams.

In recent decades, the pace of change worldwide has been meteoric and it shows no sign of slowing. New innovations in information technologies and the growing sophistication of the Internet, together with advances in medicine, physics and psychology, to name a few, are changing our understanding of how everything — including the human mind itself — works.

And this changed understanding is affecting every area of our lives.

The purpose of *Pre-school Parenting Secrets: Talking with the Sky* is to empower you, the parent, to instil in young children, the learning habits and the confident mindset of future champions.

If we want our children to succeed in the 21st Century, we must ensure that they are adequately prepared — that they have both the self-confidence and the skills to succeed in the world created by the Information Revolution.

The strategies we outline in the chapters that follow draw on studies from a wide variety of disciplines, including research into the nature and development of creative intelligence.

Championship in the 21st Century will require the twin abilities of active creativity and high-level social skills, and the exciting thing is that these are skills for which most pre-school children already possess great potential.

If we are aware, we can nurture and strengthen this potential during the early years, within the protective environment of the home. If we do this effectively, we can avoid it being unnecessarily — and prematurely — crushed by the pressures of the world beyond.

Expanding the 'Comfort Zone'

To judge a bamboo plant's progress only according to what we see on the surface is to ignore the massive preparation that has occurred under the ground.

In the same way, to think that the activities outlined in this series are 'just play' or 'just fun' is to miss the complex cognitive growth taking place beneath the surface. It is pointless to judge a child by the evidence of surface learning at a young age. To do so is to completely miss the point of early childhood learning. As a society, we are hung up on assessment and evidence. We seem to work on the assumption that if we can't measure it, it doesn't exist.

Albert Einstein — the absolute epitome of the creative thinker — summed up the fallacy of this mindset, on a sign which he hung in his office at Princeton. It read:

Not everything that counts can be counted, and not everything that can be counted counts.

Many people believe that promoting children's growth requires 'throwing them in at the deep end' — pushing or forcing them out of their comfort zone and beyond their previous achievements.

Sadly, this belief is outdated for a number of developmental reasons — and especially for this age group.

While it is true that, as human beings, we learn little if we stay within our comfort zone, the good news is that, for children, as long as it is connected to an enjoyable experience, we can gradually extend the comfort zone — and therefore the learning potential — without their being aware of just how far they have come. And because experience is the true teacher, once they have moved beyond the old boundaries, they rarely, if ever, go backwards.

Learning changes the very structure of our brain. Learn something new, something beyond your previous experience, and you begin to think differently. You are not, and can never again be, the same person.

In the end, it is far more effective to expand a child's boundaries gradually through carefully structured activities. Completing the activities outlined in this series expands a child's comfort zone — often without the child even noticing.

With the right strategies, all children can learn by using the natural, intuitive abilities with which they were born. This approach forms a secure and solid platform upon which to build the future learning behaviours — especially creativity, logical thinking and problem-solving — which will lead to sustainable success in Primary School and in later life.

This is the active principle behind each strategy developed for **Pre-school Parenting Secrets: Talking with the Sky**.

> **Expand a child's world and you expand that child's mind.**
>
> **Create a new understanding and you lay the foundations for a lifetime of future understanding.**
>
> **Open a gate and the road beyond goes on forever...**

The 'Key Roots'

Just like the Bamboo, the successful pre-school learner develops 'key roots' that will support future growth spurts in learning and championship.

Importantly, this does not involve drilling a young child in specific topics with repetition, flash-cards and rote-learning — a common approach, which is boring and frustrating for young children, and ultimately pointless.

> **Young children are experiential learners, which is to say, they learn by doing — by hands-on experience and experimentation — and by tying that learning to positive emotions.**

Each activity outlined in this series is designed to develop competence in one or more key areas of a child's development. These strategies are built around physical activities, structured game-playing, supportive interaction and, above all, FUN.

So, don't expect to find advice on how to turn your child into a human calculator or a robotic reading machine before s/he enters kindergarten. There are expensive books and programmes out there eager and willing to offer the promise of producing, in your child, the next ten-year-old Nobel Prize winner.

There is a huge difference between genius and a Champion Mindset. Genius occurs spontaneously and is at the present time unexplained and unable to be duplicated. A Champion Mindset can also appear spontaneously in lucky individuals, but the work of Professor Allan Snyder FRS, at the Centre for the Mind, Sydney, shows us that it can also be learned — and taught.

What we offer, in this book, is a different way of thinking about your child's development and some easy-to-use activities to lay the foundations — the root-system — which will support the development of your future champion.

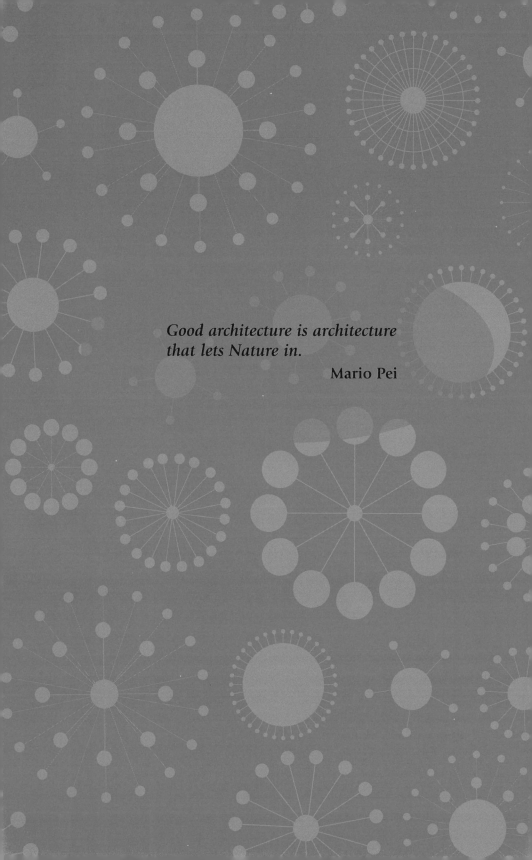

Good architecture is architecture that lets Nature in.

Mario Pei

CHAPTER ONE

THE SCIENCE

What Research Tells Us About the Needs of a Child

SACHA

Brian writes:

Recently, I received an invitation to Sacha's wedding. Sacha is a beautiful, talented and confident young woman of 25, whom I have had the privilege of knowing for almost 20 years.

Looking at her face, smiling back at me from the photo on the wedding invitation took me back to the first time I met Sacha...

It was October 1992, in Sydney, Australia.

Amanda B. sat opposite me in a comfortable chair, beside a picture window that looked out onto a lovingly-tended garden in full Spring bloom.

Amanda and her husband Greg were new friends. I had met them through work and we had connected instantly — as sometimes happens in life — but this was the first time I had been to their house.

Amanda smiled as she gazed across the room to where her daughter, Sacha, knelt, her dolls arranged into a row, feeding each one individually, from an imaginary bowl.

Sacha was a pretty seven-year-old, with blonde ringlets and striking grey blue eyes, that gave the impression she was looking right through you. When we were introduced, a few minutes earlier, she had said hello, politely, but she had made no attempt to shake my hand when I offered it.

Then she'd turned and continued playing, as if I had ceased to exist.

Amanda and her husband Greg were English. They had arrived from London a year earlier to begin a new life 'down under', with Sacha and one-year-old James who was asleep in a cot in the next room.

'She still finds it hard to mother them,' Amanda observed, more to herself than to me, as she watched her daughter playing. 'The dolls, I mean,' she added, as she realised that I might not have been on her wavelength. 'But at least she is caring for them now. When we first brought her home, she didn't even look at them. She didn't know how to play, or what a hug was. It was heart-breaking.'

Sacha had come to live with Amanda and Greg at the age of four. She had been brought up in two different Romanian orphanages from the time she was no more than a few days old.

'They told me they'd done their best,' Greg shared once, 'but the problems were so huge. Poverty, disease... Too many kids, and too few resources.' He shook his head, as if trying to dislodge the memory. 'Most of the kids had been abandoned by their desperate parents, and the official response was to... warehouse them in these huge buildings, with unqualified staff to look after them. By the time we adopted her, she'd spent most of her first four years imprisoned in her cot, with almost no human contact. It's amazing she's come out of it so well.'

For Sacha, 'so well' meant that she was, at the age of seven, beginning to respond to people other than her adoptive parents, that she would occasionally speak more than three words together, and that she could play with dolls, and help Amanda care for James.

Children from situations similar to those experienced by Sacha almost invariably suffer from what psychologists call 'developmental delays' — especially in the area of emotional response — and often, those 'delays' become permanent. Not surprising, when you consider that they spent their formative years without the normal sensory stimulation and person-to-person experiences that the brain — including the emotional brain — needs, to 'wire itself up' for the most common human behaviours.

The less nurturing the environment, the more pronounced the developmental delays. In the case of the Romanian orphanages of the 1980s, the 'production-line' approach to addressing the orphans' basic physical needs kept them alive, but it denied them the human contact which is so essential for normal brain development.

Unlike hundreds of other children from those institutions, Sacha was lucky. Greg was a clinical psychologist, and Amanda was a passionate primary school teacher, who took four years off work to spend time with Sacha, home-schooling her and giving her the one-on-one attention she so desperately needed.

'Nothing you can do,' she told me, between sips of her coffee, 'can make up for what she lost in those first crucial years. The emotional foundations are so fragile that for every two steps you go forward, you slip back at least one. Sometimes, it's like trying to climb up a muddy hillside in a rainstorm, carrying a bag of cement on your back. But you keep going. What else can you do?'

She placed the cup down on the table before her, and stood up, staring out of the window, as if the peace of the garden beyond the glass could absorb the remembered pain.

Finally, she turned back to face me.

'Then there are the breakthroughs that make it all worthwhile,' she continued, the smile returning to her face. 'Like the first time she kissed me back.'

'I'd spent hours, every day, just holding her; keeping up a constant one-sided conversation, rubbing her hair, and her skin, blowing on her face, kissing her cheeks or her eyes, or her head — anything to make up for those years of deprivation. Then one day, she looked up at me, and without any warning, she sat up and kissed me on the cheek. I cried with sheer joy for at least an hour. Of course, she didn't do it again for a couple of weeks, but that was a special day.'

I watched Amanda wipe her eye, as the memory played itself out. 'You do what you can,' she said, at last. 'And wait for the golden moments. That one was 24 carat...'

Today, Sacha has an honours degree and a burgeoning career in public relations. She spends her weekends partying and playing netball, and I am sitting here looking at her smiling back at me from the invitation to her upcoming wedding.

It is the happy ending that her parents prayed for during the difficult early years — the one that they worked so hard to achieve. Sacha is living proof of the power of connection — and the vital importance of creating a secure attachment with our children.

Marcel Proust once wrote:

Let us be grateful to people who make us happy; they are the charming gardeners who make our souls blossom.

Fortunately, few children in our prosperous and privileged society experience anything like the traumas that marked Sacha's early years.

As parents, we all try to make our children happy, to give them the support and the confidence, to grow — but, sometimes, we receive mixed messages about how to fulfil this, the most important of all parental roles.

Notice that Proust doesn't say 'Let us be grateful to people who buy us things', or even 'Let us be grateful to people who educate us'. Rather, he looks at the most basic need of a human being — to be happy.

And for young children, indeed for all of us, to be happy is to belong — to feel a secure attachment with those whose role is to 'make our souls blossom'.

As the anonymous observer points out:

Children spell LOVE, T.I.M.E.

Time to connect. Time to feel close. Time to share the experiences that shape their understanding — of themselves and their place in the world.

But such time is not measured in minutes and hours — it is measured in moments. The time we share with our children should be assessed not by its duration, but by its quality — by the memories it produces.

This chapter looks at our children's most basic needs, and how easy it is to fulfil them — even in our busy lives.

A: Attachment and Bonding

Planting the Seed

> **Happiness held is the seed. Happiness shared is the flower.**
> **— Sign in a Friend's Flower Garden**

The Power of a Hug

Just about every parent knows how much their children adore being hugged. This simple expression of love for a child is at the heart of a hugely significant and influential area of research by psychologists known as 'Attachment Theory'.

What Is Attachment Theory?

Attachment Theory seeks to explain the special emotional relationship between a care-giver and a child. That relationship involves the exchange of comfort and care, making a child feel secure and safe. Secure attachment to a child's primary care-givers (usually the parents) gives that child solid emotional and psychological foundations for life.

Psychologist John Bowlby[2] is the world's best-known researcher of Attachment Theory. Bowlby described attachment as a *'lasting psychological connectedness between human beings'*. He found that children who formed a secure attachment with their parents at an early age have the following characteristics in common:

- higher self-esteem
- greater academic success
- increased ability to manage their impulses and their feelings
- increased ability to cope with difficulties
- positive relationships with parents and other care-givers — and with authority figures

In 1988 Vera Fahlberg's research on Attachment[3] supported Bowlby's. She found that as securely-attached children grow, they are better able to:

- attain their full intellectual potential
- sort out what they perceive and understand

- think logically
- develop a conscience
- become self-reliant
- cope with stress and frustration
- handle fear and worry
- develop future relationships
- reduce jealousy

Studies have shown that securely-attached children are less disruptive, less aggressive, and more mature. They are better able to concentrate, and therefore learn more effectively and more successfully.

What Is Bonding?

Bowlby's extensive research revealed that the best way to achieve a strong attachment with a child is through what he called 'bonding experiences'. The acts of holding, rocking, singing, feeding, gazing, kissing and other nurturing behaviours involved in caring for infants and young children are all bonding experiences.

This means that, in childhood, the *quantity* and the *quality* of the time spent with a child is critically important. Bonding experiences include face-to-face interactions, eye contact, physical proximity, touch and other primary sensory experiences such as smell, sound and taste.

While it is always valuable for parents to spend as much time as possible with their children, just being in the same room with a child is not necessarily a bonding experience. A bonding experience typically has four elements:

1. *The parent is paying attention to the child.*

2. *Parent and child are interacting in some way by having verbal and/or non-verbal exchanges.*

3. *Positive emotions are experienced in rapport between the parent and child. Being 'in rapport' is most easily defined as connecting or sharing — as being 'in tune' with one another at an emotional level.*

4. *Bonding often involves touch, such as hugging.*

Parents can use these four elements as a rule-of-thumb checklist to determine if they are engaging in a bonding experience with their child — but if bonding is truly taking place, you won't need a checklist. You will know it.

A bonding experience can last for hours if the parent and child are engaging in an activity together, or a few seconds if they are exchanging a kiss or hug.

Scientists believe the most important factor in creating attachment is positive physical contact such as hugging, massaging, holding and rocking.

It should be no surprise that holding, gazing, smiling, kissing, singing, and laughing all cause specific neurochemical responses in the brain. Massaging or hugging your child decreases the stress hormones of both parent and child, and has been shown to significantly improve children's behaviour.[4]

These neurochemical activities contribute to the normal organisation of brain systems which are responsible for attachment — and other important developmental functions.

How Much Bonding Is Enough?

One of the most common questions we are asked, whenever we talk to parents of pre-school children, relates to how much bonding time is enough.

This is a bit of a 'how-long-is-a-piece-of-string?'-type question and we are always reluctant to place a rigid timeframe on bonding experiences, for fear of creating the wrong impression.

Different children require different amounts of bonding time, and besides, the quality of the experience is rarely time-related.

A few seconds of true rapport can be worth an hour of enforced, by-the-numbers, 'they-told-me-this-whole-Bonding-thing-was-a-Good-Idea-so-I-suppose-I-should-do-it' time-sharing.

Bonding is not something to be timetabled, like housework or grocery-shopping, and it amused us to read how one Japanese-based 'right-brain' training programme, with more than a few bizarre ideas, actually stipulates the number of seconds that parents should hold a hug with their child. This is an example of 'pseudo-science' gone crazy.

David writes:

I remember a time when I was six years old. It was my first week at school and as the bell was about to ring for the end of school, the monsoon rain was pouring heavily and the sky was crowded with thick black clouds, and illuminated by sudden bolts of lightning.

I was a little scared, and for some reason, at that moment I really missed my father. I remember praying, "Please, please let my dad come and pick me up today…"

In those days my parents were working very hard, building their business, and I would be picked up by our helper, and as I prayed, I felt as if the dark clouds which boiled in the sky above were all around me.

I watched through the rain, the chaos of many adults rushing to pick up my school-mates, and just when I had resigned myself to the fact that my father was probably too busy to come, I suddenly saw my dad in his yellow raincoat, pushing his scooter through the crowd. I remember saying, "Thank you! Thank you!"

All I remember after that is sitting on the back of the scooter, beneath my dad's yellow raincoat, hugging him so tightly that I could feel the warmth of his body against my left cheek.

Many years later, I was a father of two children myself. My dad and I were up late one night talking, and I shared this story with him.

At that moment, I saw my elderly Chinese father — who rarely showed his emotions — shed tears. He had never realised how much this moment had meant to me. In fact, he didn't remember the incident at all.

What I learned from this is that if these critical bonding moments can happen by 'accident' — and yet mean so much to a child and help shape the adult he will become — then imagine how powerful it would be to craft these moments with our own children.

What I also realised was that these moments can happen 'out of the blue', at any time of the day — and that it is our responsibility, as parents, to seize them.

A saying which resonates from some time in my childhood runs:

"An ordinary person waits for opportunities and a good person looks for opportunities — while a great person creates his own opportunities."

The myth is that in our busy lives, we do not have the time. But it is not about 'time' alone. The truth is that it is about 'moments'.

Opportunities are like buses, but many people just sit and watch them go by.

How many special moments with your parents do you remember from your childhood? How many will your children remember from theirs with you?

Opportunities for bonding arise in all manner of ways — often without warning. Cooking a meal, vacuuming the house, washing the car or even sitting knitting can all become bonding experiences, if you share the experience in a fun, loving way, with lots of tactile attention and eye contact, verbal encouragement, fun and laughter.

Then there are the quiet times which you set aside to just be close and share with your child. Talking about shared experiences, reading a book together, singing a song or sharing a poem — these and a thousand similar moments can bring you closer together, as they build your child's confidence and sense of belonging.

> **Even half an hour a day will make a world of difference to your child — and to you! It will ease your stress and has, for many parents we have worked with, become the period of the day they most look forward to.**

It is a basic principle of the human emotional make-up, that when we make another human being happy — especially a child, and more especially our own child — changes take place within our brains, which release endorphins and other neurochemicals, making us feel happier, less stressed and more relaxed.

What if I have More than One Child?

If you have more than one child, there are times when shared bonding experiences can occur — such as playing games together, spending half an hour in bed on the weekends, and countless other possible scenarios.

These shared bonding experiences are vitally important for establishing the cohesive family unit and strengthening sibling bonds.

> **This being said, however, as parents, we must still make time for some 'one-on-one' quality bonding time with each child as an individual.**

This is especially important for the older child, particularly if there is only a small gap between siblings. Often, the older child has had to adjust from being the centre of adult attention to being the 'big' brother or sister, and watching a 'usurper' come in and take the emotional spotlight.

Regular bonding time with parents can ease the sense of loss and show the child that s/he is still 'special' and important — especially if s/he is also given a role in caring for the younger child.

Are All Fun Family Experiences Bonding Experiences?

The simple answer to this question is 'Yes... and no'.

All family recreational experiences are important, and they all strengthen the ties which bind the family together, but different activities will contain a different balance of the bonding elements.

A trip to a theme park, for example, may certainly become a well-loved and treasured memory, but in terms of a bonding experience, from a purely psychological perspective, it may well lack the personal contact elements we referred to above.

If a child plays or rides, and the parents stand and watch, even if they wave as the child rides by, the experience may better be classed as a shared family entertainment.

The same may be said of taking children to see a movie. In a psychological sense, the child has more of a bonding experience with Nemo, Cinderella or Despereaux than they do with Mum or Dad.

So, does this mean we shouldn't do all these things with our children?

Of course we should!

Such shared family events have their own place in building the complex nurturing relationship between parent and child. They provide novel experiences and enjoyable memories, which help create the complex fabric of childhood — which, in turn, helps mould the adult experience of the world beyond childhood.

They are also an excellent source of future bonding moments — where the excitement of the ride, or the story of the film can be woven into conversations and games, where re-tellings and role-plays can be teased out of the experiences, with opportunities to expand creativity and strengthen rapport.

The lesson is that every experience — shared or otherwise — is the material from which bonding is forged. The more pleasant experiences the family has shared, the more the future bonding opportunities flow.

Characteristics of Children and Adults with Secure Attachment

Securely-attached children become secure adults. Below is a table, adapted from the work of John Bowlby.[5] It describes the behaviours of securely-attached children and how these behaviours evolve as they grow to adulthood.

Children	Adults
1. Able to separate from parent with confidence	1. Have trusting and lasting relationships
2. Seek comfort from parents when frightened	2. Tend to have good self-esteem
3. Return of parents is met with positive emotions	3. Comfortable sharing feelings with friends and partners
4. Prefers parents to strangers	4. Seek out social support

How Do Parents of Securely-Attached Children Behave?

Parents of securely-attached children tend to play more with their children. Additionally, these parents react more quickly to their children's needs and are generally more responsive than parents of insecurely-attached children.

Of course, bonding with children is different from spoiling them.

While being there and sharing time and experiences are crucial, this does not mean submitting to every whim of the child. Nor does it mean compensating for a lack of attention by attempting to buy happiness with gifts.

Research worldwide shows that as society has grown more materially wealthy — as more 'things' have become available for children — the incidence of depression and emotional problems has also increased.

Remember the Reverend Jesse Jackson's perceptive and often-quoted observation:

Your children need your presence more than your presents.

Bonding — the Easiest Parenting Task of All!

Of all the things parents must do to take care of their children, bonding is not only the easiest, but it is the least expensive and the most enjoyable. And of all the things you, as a parent, can do to make the greatest impact on your child's future happiness and success, bonding with your child to create a secure attachment has by far the greatest impact.

It all starts with a simple hug...

To Do...

1. Consider the bonding experiences described above. How often do you consider it necessary to engage in such experiences with your child/ren?

2. Bonding can occur during such activities as:
   a. Reading a book
   b. Cooking together
   c. Playing a game together
   d. Going for a walk
   e. Having a chat, and asking your children how they think and feel

   Add in some more activities that you currently do with your children that you regard as bonding experiences.

❧

B: A Hierarchy of Needs

First Things First — I Can't Be a Genius if I'm Hungry!

> **Bread feeds the body indeed, but flowers feed also the soul.**
>
> **— The Qur'an**

Think of the survival needs of humans who lived 20,000 years ago.

Each day, the first priority would be finding food and water. The next priority would be to find or make a shelter that provided protection from the weather and safety from wild animals. These are the basic necessities of human survival.

It would also then have been important for early man to belong to a family or a tribe, as humans have a strong need to belong to social groups. From an evolutionary stand-point, such a drive would have a high 'survivability' factor, as in a dangerous environment, there is safety in numbers.

By satisfying the same genetically coded need for belonging, modern humans feel valued and can develop self worth and esteem.

> **It may surprise you to discover that in 20,000 years, basic human needs have not really changed.**
>
> **Our needs also seem to naturally present themselves in an order, from basic physical needs up through the more complex emotional and psychological needs.**

Over 65 years ago, psychologist Abraham Maslow created a model to describe this phenomenon and called it the Hierarchy of Needs.[6]

Maslow's Hierarchy of Needs is highly respected and widely applied in the fields of psychology, education and business.

It is also the model that effective school teachers understand and refer to in relation to a child's ability to socialise, learn and achieve at school. But more than that, it's a model that effective parents can use to nurture their children — from birth to adulthood — and beyond.

All That a Human Being Needs Can Be Found in a Pyramid!

Abraham Maslow published the Hierarchy of Needs in his paper *A Theory of Human Motivation*, in 1943. His theory states that humans need to meet their 'basic needs' of food, shelter and safety before they can achieve 'higher needs' such as belonging, self-esteem and self-actualisation.

It makes sense that if we have plenty to eat and are safe, loved and supported, we can truly thrive and achieve our life's ambitions.

Maslow's Hierarchy of Needs

There are a number of different versions of the Hierarchy of Needs model. We have selected a simple version which demonstrates the model in a clear way.

The diagram above shows Maslow's Hierarchy of Needs as a pyramid. The more basic needs are placed at the bottom with the 'higher' needs of self-actualisation and transcendence at the top — because they can only be achieved when all other needs are satisfied.

Self-actualisation for human beings occurs when they are achieving at their best in relationships and learning. Even very young children are capable of this level of achievement.

Transcendence is when we feel part of something larger, beyond ourselves. It is the highest state which a human being is capable of achieving, and although young children cannot conceptualise something beyond their own immediate experience, at their age, feeling valued as a part of the family is a good approximation.

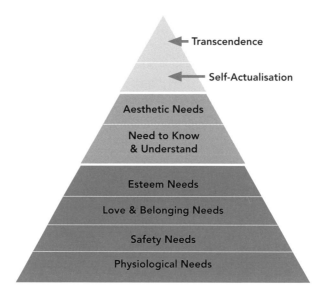

But What Do All These Labels Mean?

Scientists — and psychologists are no exception — love to categorise; to gather together a whole range of ideas (in this case, 'Needs') under one heading. So, to make it simpler, we will outline some of the key elements in each category.

Remember, as you go through them, that Maslow was talking about all human beings from the youngest to the oldest. Some of the elements he discussed — like 'sexual intimacy' or 'security of employment' — are pretty much irrelevant for young children, so we have left them out of this summary, concentrating on those elements that are most essential to your young child.

What is really amazing is just how many are still applicable...

Starting from the bottom of the pyramid — the most basic needs — we have:

1. **Physiological:** breathing; water; food; sleep; health and the excretion of wastes.

2. **Safety:** security of body; freedom from fear or pain; security of family, resources (belongings) and health.

3. **Love/Belonging:** to belong to and receive positive responses from family, friends and (sometimes) pets.

4. **Esteem:** self-esteem; confidence; recognition of achievement by others (especially parents); personal sense of achievement; respect of others and respect by others.

5. **Need to Know and Understand:** discovering; experimenting; experiencing new things; re-experiencing previously discovered things; mastery; acceptance of facts; making sense and making connections.

6. **Aesthetic:** As human beings, we respond both logically and emotionally — both through our conscious thoughts and through our senses. [Aesthetics refers to how we make sense of our emotional and sensory responses — how we 'join the dots' to deepen our understanding and enjoyment of the world around us — of what makes something aesthetically satisfying. Developing an aesthetic response to our environment is an essential step towards creativity — to 'joining our own dots'.]

7. **Self-Actualisation:** creativity; spontaneity; problem-solving; ethical behaviour (yes, with experience and guidance, a young child is capable of determining right from wrong) and social behaviour.

8. **Transcendence:** the security of belonging and contributing to the extended family or some other group. In young children, this can take the form of contribution to the wider community. It could involve helping a neighbour or helping parents with charity work, for example.

Maslow explained that we must satisfy a lower need before the need above it on the pyramid becomes a 'driver' of behaviour.

For example, if a child is hungry, thirsty, lacking sleep, sick or constipated, nothing above the bottom level of the pyramid will be of the remotest importance to him or her.

Likewise, if children feel unsafe, neglected or insecure in their home situation, they will lack a sense of love and belonging. This will lead, eventually, to lower self-esteem.

Under these circumstances, there will be no drive to experiment or learn. The child will experience a lack of the self-confidence, and the will to be creative and solve problems will be diminished. Unless a child has a positive self-image, derived from attention to the lower segments of the 'Needs Pyramid', s/he cannot devote the attention and energy required to succeed in any endeavour, particularly schooling.[7]

However, when the physical, emotional and social needs of children are being satisfied, then they are free to make sense of the world at large. The drive to know and understand, and the ability to enjoy, aesthetically, everything the world has to offer, is strong even in very young children, and it is the basis of all effective learning behaviours.

Once the basic needs have been satisfied, our role, as parents, is to nurture inquisitiveness and the sheer joy of experiencing new things, by modelling, for young children, the excitement and wonder that exist within every new experience.

Attachment, Bonding and Maslow

Attachment theory and bonding mesh perfectly with Maslow's Hierarchy of Needs. When children's primary needs are met consistently in a nurturing way by a parent, children learn that they are important and that they can count on others.

When they develop secure attachment through bonding experiences, children feel more confident about exploring the world around them. They can concentrate on — and succeed in — learning, and develop relationships with others.

So Many Needs!

By now, you may be thinking that this all makes good common sense. As parents, we need to ensure that our children are fed, have a safe place to live, belong to a well connected and functional family and feel a strong sense of self worth and esteem in order for them to thrive.

Easy? Of course it is! We promise that nothing in this book will be too difficult.

Parenting is a huge responsibility — but it doesn't have to be an onerous one! As long as we understand the need for a balance between all levels of the needs hierarchy, we can help our children learn to balance their own approach to life.

Of course, parenting would be a breeze if all we had to do was provide our children with food and a secure place to live! The challenge for us, as parents, is to give our children a strong emotional foundation, to enable them to cope and thrive through the minefield of life's events, and, ultimately, to follow their dreams.

The good news is that the basic needs are usually the easiest to address — especially for young children. This means that we can easily lay strong foundations — a base upon which to build. And, as with the pyramids of antiquity (which still stand today), a strong base creates a solid structure upon which a balanced life can be constructed.

SEEs and Maslow's Needs

It's an inescapable fact that occurrences happen in the lives of children — positive or negative — which are outside of their control. Why should they be any different to their parents?

These occurrences are sometimes called Significant Emotional Events (SEEs). Examples of SEEs include, among many others:

- starting school

- moving house

- taking an exam

- a long sickness or major accident/injury

- going on holiday

- parental separation and divorce

- death of a member of the family or a pet

- loss of a friend

Any one of these events can threaten a child's sense of belonging, security and safety. When parents are armed with the knowledge of how the Hierarchy of Needs model works, they are better able to understand and support their children through life's SEEs.

By focussing on the 'need' that has been compromised as a result of the SEE, parents have the tools to be able to help their children return to a state of self-actualisation faster.

For example, if a child has become lost and frightened, restoring a sense of safety and belonging may require increasing the time spent engaged in bonding experiences. Most parents would do this instinctively, of course — picking the child up, hugging and comforting him or her, until the fear subsides.

Other SEEs — like starting school, or a major trauma — while they require more substantial intervention, still follow the same principle. A conscious awareness of the child's needs is the first step towards addressing them.

To Do...

Consider what you already do, and what you would like to do more of, to meet your child's needs. You will find that the strategies for the earlier needs are easier to identify, but be tough on yourself and see if you can come up with strategies which will work for you and your child, to help facilitate the higher-order needs.

Rather than limiting yourself here, you may find it useful to assign a few pages in a notebook to each of the needs, so that you can really let your head go with ideas.

Remember: As you move through the book, you will discover, in yourself, skills that you may have forgotten you possess. Return to this exercise as often as you like, to add new insights.

Needs:

a. PHYSIOLOGICAL — *breathing, water, food, sleep, health*

Do at present	Would like to do more of
Example: Health. Our busy lifestyle means we sometimes settle for takeaway 2 or 3 times a week.	*Example:* Set aside time to plan and shop for the week's meals in advance so that we're sure our family gets the fruit and vegetables we need.

b. SAFETY — *family security, physical safety*

Do at present	Would like to do more of
Example: My son is afraid of dogs, and the dog next-door sometimes gets out and runs into our yard. This causes my son not to feel safe in our home.	*Example:* Ask my neighbours to fix their fence to keep their dog in, as well as find a way to have my son overcome his fear of dogs, perhaps through a counsellor.

c. LOVE/BELONGING — *sense of belonging and positive responses from family, friends and peers*

Do at present	Would like to do more of
Example: I love my children but I'm not sure if I often tell them so.	*Example:* Be conscious to tell my children I love them every day.

Needs:

d. ESTEEM — *self-esteem, confidence, recognition, respect for and by others*

Do at present	Would like to do more of
Example: I often say to my child "You're fantastic" but I don't really go into detail, so maybe it doesn't seem genuine.	**Example:** Tell my child specific things I appreciate. Yesterday after dinner my son took his plate to the kitchen without being asked to, so I should have said, "Well done on taking your plate to the kitchen. You're good at helping out."

e. AESTHETIC — *experimenting and sharing sensory and aesthetic experiences*

Do at present	Would like to do more of
Example: We'll walk to the park but I have noticed myself saying "Come on" when my daughter stops to look at a flower or plant.	**Example:** Slow the walk down a bit and share my daughter's experience, and talk to her about the plants and flowers — feel them, smell them.

Needs:
f. SELF-ACTUALISATION — *creativity, spontaneity, problem solving, ethical and social behaviour*

Do at present	Would like to do more of
Example: My son loves to use old cartons and packaging to make things but I find myself putting them in the bin before he sees them because he makes such a mess!	**Example:** See this as creativity, tolerate the temporary mess (take a deep breath!). Perhaps put a 'making-table' in a corner of the lounge room and tell him that this is the place to make things, instead of all over the house.

g. TRANSCENDENCE — *security and contribution to extended family and wider community*

Do at present	Would like to do more of
Example: I visit my grandmother once a month but I have tended not to take my children along because she's frail and I'm worried they might be rowdy.	**Example:** Foster a sense of caring for our elderly family members in my children. Perhaps we could bake biscuits together and my children could bring them to my grandma, and then I could talk to them about speaking softly and sitting down when we're there.

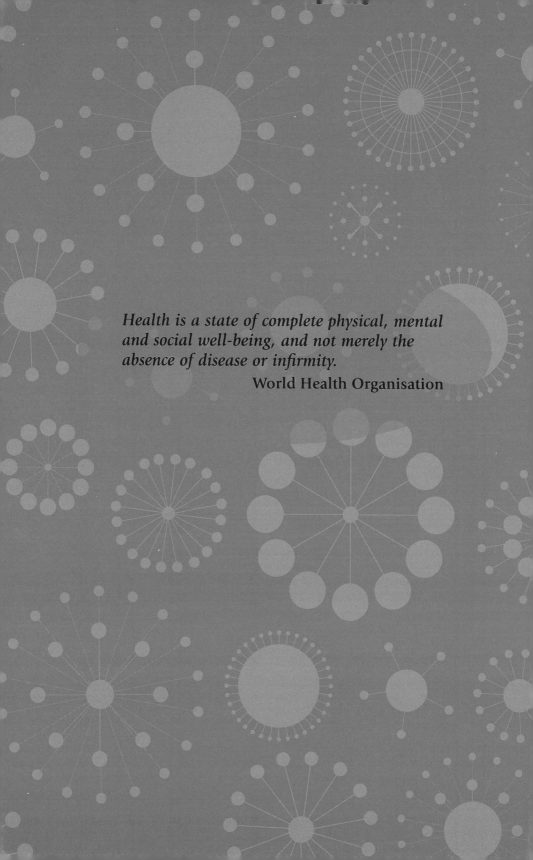

Health is a state of complete physical, mental and social well-being, and not merely the absence of disease or infirmity.

World Health Organisation

THE PHYSICAL NEEDS

Understanding Your Child's Basic Physical Needs

(Healthy Development through Sensible Decision-Making)

TYLER

Tyler D wakes up and looks around at the shadows that inhabit his room.

It is still dark outside, but the night-light is on, and the flat panel of the TV glows blue, with the DVD's screen-saver blinking slowly on and off and sliding randomly from one section of the screen to another. He stares at it for a few seconds, while his brain emerges from the fog of waking.

Late last night, as he drifted slowly to sleep, the movie had not quite played itself out, and he remembers very little about it — except that it was funny and colourful and involved a rat in a French restaurant.

He searches for the remote and finds it tangled in among the blankets. He points it towards the screen and presses 'play', waiting a few seconds for the machine to respond. Then he lies back against the pillow and begins to watch.

As the opening credits appear, the clock on the wall above the door reads five-thirty, but he doesn't see it. And even if he did, Tyler cannot tell the time.

Because Tyler is only four years old.

'Trying to get Tyler to sleep was killing us,' his father confided in friends at a recent dinner party, but then his face lit up. 'But now we've found the perfect solution. No more tantrums. No more complaints. We put on a DVD and before you know it, he's drifting off. You know how bad I am at reading bedtime stories? Well, the movie is much better than a picture book anyway, so while he watches, the TV tells him his bedtime story. It's the perfect solution!'

Through the bedroom window, the first rays of sunlight are just beginning to show over the distant horizon, but Tyler doesn't notice. The frenetic movement of the animated creatures on the screen in front of him has captured his focus. In two hours' time, when the movie finishes, he will climb out of bed and make his way to his parents' bedroom to wake them.

And they, being the loving parents everyone knows them to be, will get up and begin preparing breakfast – Tyler's favourite sugar-frosted corn flakes and strawberry pop-tarts.

'What can I say?' his mother has been heard to ask, with a slightly resigned shrug of her shoulders. 'He has a sweet tooth. Takes after his father. Besides, he burns it off. Never saw such a hyperactive kid. I don't know how the poor teachers are going to cope when he gets to school. You don't know,' she sometimes continues, 'what an ordeal it is, trying to get him to eat vegetables. But look at him. Does he look malnourished to you?'

For now, Tyler is content. The cartoon mayhem flashes before his rapt gaze, the room is warm and the bed is comfortable.

What more could a young child ask for?

What More, Indeed?

The problem with pre-schoolers — with children of all ages, for that matter — is that they don't know what to ask for. That they don't even know what is good for them.

Nature has not equipped human beings with an inbuilt instinct for 'right-thinking' at an early age. Young children are sensory-emotional beings, with very little capacity for considered responses.

Which is as it should be.

Without the life experience which informs our adult decision-making, they are, at best, 'apprentice thinkers'. They learn from their mistakes and make sense of the world through trial and error.

> **Our responsibility, as parents and carers, is to provide the experiences — and the guidance — to help them make the world make sense.**

It is also our duty to make all the important decisions — the ones which will affect their health and well-being — with the best interests of the children in mind. And this includes making ourselves aware of any and all factors which will improve the decisions we make.

It is disturbing, therefore, that a growing number of parents, following the philosophy of 'anything-for-an-easy-life', are leaving many of the day's most important decisions (on nutrition, sleep patterns and social behaviour, to name just three) in the hands of their media-saturated under-fives.

Make no mistake. Decisions on what a child eats, how much she sleeps, and how he interacts with others, are vitally important. They provide the physical, psychological — and neurological — foundations for behaviours which the individual will maintain throughout life, and they can also be essential for a child's healthy physical development in the crucial early years.

Unfortunately, pre-schoolers are experts at one thing. From birth, they have been instinctively refining the art of getting what they want in the moment.

They seem to know instinctively what behaviour they can display which will make their parents respond in the manner they want them to.

As they gradually grasp the concept that they are an independent person with their own will, pre-school children employ strategies to get or do the things that they want. And their energy for persistence is unrivalled — especially by tired and over-worked parents!

Pre-school children have a variety of strategies suitable for all manner of situations.

It might be coming out of their bedroom 20 times in an hour at bedtime, because they know that, eventually, mum will let them fall asleep beside her on the sofa.

Or it might be spitting out their food in a dramatised vomit to get out of eating their broccoli.

Whatever the stratagem, they have the persistence to keep it up until the goal is achieved. Even if the result is — from a mature, adult perspective — an unsatisfactory one.

It may be easier in the short-term to give in, but the long-term consequences of such a capitulation can be serious.

Giving in can, in the moment, seem like the better of two evils — the easier decision — but remember this truism:

For the parent of a pre-schooler, there is no such thing as an easy decision — nor, for that matter, is there such a thing as a hard decision.

There are only decisions based on careful consideration of the long-term needs and requirements of the child, or decisions based on short-term expediency.

Rarely do the two coincide.

Restating the Obvious

This section looks at some of children's most fundamental physical needs.

As we saw earlier, the intrinsic needs of the human being haven't changed in millennia. Unfortunately, however, in today's society — dominated as it is by the mass media — it is sometimes these more basic areas of need which present parents with the most persistent challenges.

Some of what follows may seem glaringly obvious — all children need the right food, the right amount of sleep, the right balance of laughter and challenge... Most of us could complete this list without too much trouble.

But, obvious or not, they are important. And modern life isn't easily compartmentalised. With the demands of our multi-tasking lifestyle encroaching more and more into our home life, sometimes the easy solution — the fastfood fix; the flat-screen electronic nanny — is a seductive alternative.

So, we will restate the obvious. And then, perhaps, we may discover that some of the less seductive alternatives aren't as hard as they might seem.

❧

A: Sleep Strategies for Parents

In Defence of Sleep

> **Unfortunately, there's no snooze button on a child who wants breakfast.**
> **— Paul Hignett Harrison**

Our generation has a reputation for being sleep-deprived. Did you know that in 1910, the average adult slept 9.0 hours a night? By 1975, the total had fallen to 7.5 hours. The 2002 *Sleep in America* poll,[8] conducted by the National Science Foundation (NSF), indicated that the average American adult sleeps only 6.9 hours a night.

Of course, there is no reason to believe that this is a phenomenon limited to the US. Think about the increases in work hours in the 'Asian Tigers' economies, or in Europe — or even in 'laidback' Australia — and the universal availability of 24-hour multi-channel satellite TV.

As adults, we try to squeeze as much as possible — career, social and family activities, and late-night viewing — into our busy lives, and the only way to achieve this is by sleeping less.

Unfortunately, in our quest to achieve more in one day, we may be damaging our own health, and passing our poor sleep habits on to our children, which may well jeopardise both their health and their life prospects — including their ability to learn.

So, why, exactly, is sleep so important?

Sleep, Concentration and Memory Formation

When children (and, indeed, adults) don't have enough sleep, it affects their concentration the next day and they can have problems forming effective memories.

Researchers generally accept that sleep allows neurons to 'shut down' and repair any damage done during the day. Sleep is the time when the body rids itself most effectively of the poisonous waste products which build up around cells during daytime activities.

Without the chance to repair damage and remove waste products, the neurons and other cells may not function correctly due to a build-up of toxins.

Sleep is also the time when short-term memories are converted to long-term ones, moving information from the hippocampus to the cerebral cortex. Without such transference, information can be lost, and the short-term memory becomes quickly overloaded, so that new memories cannot be effectively made.

Though it can vary from individual to individual, the human body needs a very specific period of sleep in order for this process to occur. If a person — especially a young child — gets fewer hours of sleep than needed, the system cannot complete its important work.

Growth and Repair

You can't repair or maintain a machine while it is operating at full stretch — and the body is no different. Sleep allows for 'down-time' so that the body can repair and grow.

Body and skin tissue repair takes place while we sleep. This includes repair to the UV damage done daily to the skin by exposure to sunlight. Getting enough deep sleep helps the skin repair itself.

Sleep also allows for the production and regulation of important hormones. In children, the human growth hormone (HGH) is released during deep sleep, so good sleep is essential for normal growth to occur.

Inadequate sleep can affect hormonal balance in adults as well.

Behaviours of Tired Children

Because they are growing so rapidly and learning so much, children need more sleep than adults. Sleep is vital for normal growth, brain development and a healthy immune system.

If children do not get the necessary amount of sleep, they begin to demonstrate anti-social behaviours. Sleep deprivation is linked with behavioural problems such as aggression, defiance, irritability, emotional over-reaction and hyperactivity.[9] These behaviours in children are difficult to manage at home or in learning environments.

If these facts are not enough reason to establish a healthy sleeping regime for your child, consider the following:

The sleep habits we develop at a young age significantly influence our lifelong sleep patterns.

Why is this important?

Because, in the long-term, sleep deprivation is linked, among other things, to high stress, diabetes, obesity, cardio-vascular disease, depression, stroke and immune-deficiency.

Still want to watch that midnight movie?

Tired Children Struggle Academically

Lack of sleep also affects a child's ability to succeed academically.

Children's ability to learn, concentrate, store and recall information, make decisions and solve problems is significantly reduced if they receive even one hour less sleep than is recommended for their age group.

In his book *Healthy Sleep Habits, Happy Child*,[10] Marc Weissbluth, MD, states:

School Achievement difficulties were found more often among poor sleepers compared to good sleepers... Young children who have difficulty sleeping become older children with more academic problems.

It is very important for our children's future that they receive the recommended amount of sleep for their developmental stage — especially during the pre-school years.

Better Sleepers Are Better Readers and Learners

Recent research, which is of great importance to the parents of pre-school children, indicates that the reading problems encountered by some students may in fact be traced back to memory problems occurring due to lack of sleep.

In learning to read, young children need to store and recall letters, sounds and words. If they do not receive enough sleep, their brains will not have enough time to fully form the memories from the previous day's lessons, creating gaps in their learning which lead to greater problems in future years.

An experiment conducted by Harvard Professor Matthew Walker and his colleagues in 2007[11] found that sleep-deprived students performed as much as 40 percent worse on memory testing when compared to students who had a normal night's sleep. They concluded that if a person has had a bad night's sleep, s/he is not able to commit new experiences to memory.

Giving our children enough sleep at pre-school age gives them a great head-start for learning to read and sets them up for academic success.

How Much Sleep Does My Child Need?

The *American Academy of Paediatrics Guide to Your Child's Sleep*[12] provides some helpful guidelines regarding how much sleep children need at different stages of their development:

1. **Three- to ten-year-olds need 10 to 12 hours a night**
2. **11- to 12-year-olds need about 10 hours**
3. **Teenagers need about 9 hours per night**
4. **Adults need a minimum of 7 hours, but anywhere between 7 to 9 hours**

These numbers reflect total sleep hours in a 24-hour period. If your child naps during the day, you can take that time into account when you add up the total. But remember also that due to the effect of the human circadian rhythms (how our bodies react, among other things, to the presence of light), the body chemistry alters at regular intervals during the day. At around sunset, it begins to slow down, ready for sleep, and at about 2 am, it begins to enter its 'wake-cycle' ready for the day.

> **This means that the *time a child goes to sleep is important* — not simply the number of hours.**

In terms of quality of sleep, it has been suggested that, as a rule of thumb, every hour of sleep between 7 pm and 1am is worth two hours at any other time, because the body is more prepared for sleep, and therefore gains maximum benefit from every minute.

For this reason, it is vitally important to establish a sleep-time routine which relaxes a child into sleep naturally. This *does not* include allowing children to go to sleep while watching the TV.

> No child's bedroom should have a TV in it, because TV demands both conscious and non-conscious attention, and stimulates at exactly the time when the brain should be 'winding down'.

Equally importantly, foods high in simple sugars, such as candies, sodas (especially those containing caffeine) and desserts should be kept to a minimum, especially after 3 or 4 pm, as they provide an 'energy-spike' which can act as an unnecessary stimulant for the child.

Children between the ages of three to six should generally go to bed between 7 to 9 pm and wake up ten to 12 hours later, at around 6 to 8 am.

How Do We Develop Good Sleep Habits?

In order to help a child receive enough sleep on a regular basis, a consistent 'wind-down' activity and bedtime routine is recommended.

It is suggested that children spend 30 minutes unwinding with a quiet activity such as doing a jigsaw puzzle, reading a book or quietly playing with a favourite toy before starting their bedtime routine. (Activities such as television, school work or computer games are not 'wind-down' activities!)

The wind-down activity and bedtime routine may, combined, take about an hour.

> **30 mins Wind Down + 30 mins Bedtime Routine = 1 hour**

Below are some suggestions, adapted from the work of Jennifer Wolf,[13] to help you establish a good bedtime routine:

1. Choose a bedtime for your child, and make it the same time every night (eg: 8 pm).
2. Start your 30 minute wind-down activity approximately 1 hour before bedtime (eg: 7 pm).
3. Begin your 30 minute bedtime routine approximately 30 minutes before bedtime (eg: 7.30 pm).
4. Do the same activities in the same order each night for your bedtime routine, for example, bath, put pyjamas on, brush teeth, brush hair, then reading, cuddles and then soft music. This way your child will anticipate sleep at a non-conscious level.

5. Including bath time in your bedtime routine is great because the warm water of the bath is very calming, relaxing and soothing. Adding a pure essential oil like lavender to your child's bath may also aid in their relaxation.

6. Including reading time in your bedtime routine is beneficial both emotionally (because it is a bonding activity between parent and child), and academically (because exposure to language through story during pre-school years is linked to future reading and academic success).

7. If you would like to make your child's bedtime earlier, do this gradually, by ten minutes a night until you have reached your preferred bedtime.

8. Leave the room while your child is still awake.

9. Allow soft music or a night light.

10. Remain calm when your child calls for you.

11. Reassure your child that you will come back and check on him or her during the night.

12. Impose reasonable consequences if your child refuses to go to sleep, such as, putting a favourite toy in 'time out' or limiting television time.

> ## New sleep habits take time to establish, but they lead to many future benefits.

'Wind-Down' Aids

A new habit generally takes about a month of dedicated, consistent repetition to be formed permanently. It's not easy to create a new sleep habit, but once established, the benefits to your child will last a lifetime. You will also notice calmer behaviour and more successful learning habits!

Here are some aids that you can use to help your child get used to the new routine:

1. Create a colourful sleep and wind-down routine poster with words and pictures which represent each step for your pre-school child. Your child can contribute by decorating or colouring in the poster.

2. For young children an animal hand-puppet can be used to encourage sleep. If the puppet is involved in storytime, helping to tell the story, or

comment on it, then you can create rapport between th child. As the puppet 'gets tired' it encourages the chil sleep too.

3. Playing ambience or soothing music is a wonderful way to create a relaxing, sleep-inducing atmosphere for young children. Have it playing quietly in the background, while you are going through the wind-down routine, then put it at optimum volume as you leave the room. Just make sure you don't drift off too — it's quite hypnotic!

4. In her 'must-read' book, *Reading Magic*, reading expert and beloved children's author Mem Fox of Australia suggests that if children are to become enthusiastic lifelong readers (rather than merely 'decoders'), they should experience a thousand stories before attending school. Most of these will be experienced during reading time with parents, carers or family members.

Here are five great children's books about sleep which you may find helpful — especially in the initial stages. Of course, the more books you share, the better for your pre-schooler!

1) **Remmy and the Brain Train** by James B. Maas and Guy Danella. Nearly 80% of children are sleep-deprived. This book is designed to help improve a child's sleep, daytime alertness, mood and performance.

2) **Tell Me Something Happy Before I Go To Sleep** by Joyce Dunbar with Debi Gliori (Illustrator). Willa has trouble falling asleep until her brother reminds her of all the happy things that await her in the morning.

3) **Sleep Is For Everyone** — a Let's-Read-and-Find-out Science Book by Paul Showers and Wendy Watson (Illustrator.) It discusses the importance of sleep and what happens to our brains and bodies during slumber.

4) **The Going To Bed Book** by Sandra Boynton. An assortment of animals on a boat take a bath, put on their pyjamas, brush their teeth, and exercise before going to bed.

5) **Time For Bed** by Mem Fox and Jane Dyer (Illustrator). As darkness falls parents everywhere try to get their children ready for sleep. For pre-school to grade two.

B: Healthy Nutrition

How to Encourage Your Pre-schooler to Enjoy Healthy Food

> **Ask your child what he wants for dinner, only if he's buying.**
>
> **— Fran Lebowitz**

A major part of our parenting responsibility is to ensure that our children are healthy. This includes giving our children a healthy diet and teaching them to make good food choices.

We know this is important because the food habits children develop when they are young have a strong impact on their future eating habits. Teaching pre-schoolers about good nutrition, by establishing a daily 'good food routine', can set them on the path to lifelong health.

Pre-schoolers need nutrients to provide energy, promote growth of body tissues and regulate body functions. Poor diet has been associated with the development of many of the chronic diseases such as obesity, heart disease, high blood pressure and diabetes.[14] As we know, some foods that contain artificial additives can also cause behavioural problems in children.

Teaching children to eat wisely and moderately is an investment in their future, and establishing healthy eating habits in the early years is vital to a child's future health.

Quit Clowning Around with Nutrition — Managing Marketing and the Mass Media

Traditionally, in a consumer society, success in business was defined as identifying a need, then developing a way of servicing that need. The more basic the need, the more 'essential' the service.

> **With the growth in power of the mass media, the model shifted — slightly, but significantly.**
>
> **Advertising today is designed to *redefine a need in terms of the product which has been created to satisfy it.***

Take food, for example.

As the most basic of all human needs, food is something we all must buy. After all, few people in the modern world have the capacity to grow their own. And, in most developed countries, food is available everywhere, in infinite variety.

> **With a wide variety of food available everywhere, how does an individual food supplier compete to increase its share of the market?**
>
> *By building a recognisable brand, and by redefining the basic need.*

Enter the advertising industry and — more recently — the branding industry.

Food is sustenance, but it is difficult to compete on sustenance grounds, because although sustenance is a basic need, it can be supplied by almost any food. In other words, there is no USP (Unique Selling Proposition) on a sustenance basis.

A USP is a selling point unique to a particular brand — one which will convince buyers to switch brands — and if sellers can't find one in their basic product, then they have to create one.

So, you manufacture a new, additional need and connect it to the original product. In the case of food, you can sell:

- **Quality** ('snob appeal' — 'Only superior people eat here/buy our brand')
- **Convenience** (home delivery/fastfood, etc. 'You work hard. You deserve to make your life easier. Who needs to spend hours slaving over a hot stove? Especially if we can guarantee to deliver within 30 minutes')
- **Image** ('Eat/drink this product and people will see you as fun/sexy/successful, etc.')
- **An experience** (theme restaurants, special services, etc. 'Anyone can eat, but how often do they have a meal that is also an occasion to remember?')
- **Health** (fear of the effects of inferior/adulterated foods. 'Our food is organic/preservative-free/approved by nine out of ten nutritionists polled [who just happen to be on our payroll!])

> **Or... you can be smart, and aim your advertising and branding at the most powerful, influential and vulnerable target group in the modern consumer community.**
> **CHILDREN.**

What does a red-haired clown have to do with nutrition? Very little, we would suggest.

What does he have to do with selling a brand? Everything!

The strategy is simple. Sell to the kids, and the parents (and their money) will follow. 'Fastfood' outlets are a wonderland of primary colours, cartoon characters and special offers designed to appeal to the media-saturated under-12s.

Buy this meal, and you get a 'free gift' — usually some kind of action toy related to the latest blockbuster kids' movie. A cartoon animal, a superhero or a princess — whatever will get them crowding through the doors.

And, of course, there are five models in the series, so you have to come back — and back — until you have the whole set... which sits on the furniture at home for a week until everyone has lost interest, and it is consigned to the waste bin.

We all know what they are doing, yet it works. Which wouldn't be so bad if the food were everything that a child needs.

But, of course, it is anything but.

The second commercial reality (after getting them in through the door) is to keep them coming back. The toys are a good start — as is the play area, or the décor — but it helps if the food itself is habit-forming.

Fastfoods are very high in sugar and salt, saturated with fat (all of which add to the flavour) and processed to within an inch of their nutritional lives.

Look at the following table and see where these 'foods' fit in. Their Recommended Daily Servings are listed as 'Use sparingly'.

Unfortunately, all the things which make them less than ideal as a staple diet are also all the things which keep kids — and adults — coming back for more. High-calorie, high-carbohydrate, high-fat foods burn quickly and create a 'sugar high' and a craving for a repeat dose.

To find out why, read on.

A 'junk-food' meal once a week or so is not going to do too much damage, if the rest of a child's diet is adequate and balanced, but many children eat takeaway daily — sometimes twice daily.

Is it any wonder that childhood obesity and diabetes are on the rise?

> **Of course, it doesn't have to be so.**
>
> **As the parent, it is you who make the final decisions, so you can choose to resist the media manipulation and the slick promotion, and simply say 'NO'!**

So, What Are Healthy Foods?

There are differences between cultures and countries on what is considered to be a healthy diet. The US Department of Agriculture recommends that a child between the ages of two and six years old should have a daily diet that consists of regulated portions of each major Food Group, as detailed in the table below:

Food Group	Recommended Daily Servings
Grains — Bread, Cereal, Rice, Pasta	6
Vegetables	3
Fruit	2
Dairy — Milk, Yoghurt, Cheese	2
Protein — Meat, Poultry, Fish, Dry Beans, Eggs	2
Fats, Oils, Sweets and Added Sugars	**Use sparingly**

While the US[15] recommends that children have three servings of vegetables and two servings of fruit a day, Australia recommends that they have five servings of vegetables and three servings of fruit a day.

Generally it is recommended that parents nourish their children with a wide variety of foods chosen from all the major food groups — but use fats, oils, salt and added sugars in small amounts, avoiding over-processed grains and vegetables where possible (eg: choose whole-grain or multi-grain over white bread).

A sample daily food menu which incorporates the Australian recommendations of food group portions is provided on page 80.

A Word about Carbs...

Carbohydrates are an essential part of a balanced diet for all of us — including our children — but like anything else in life, more of a good thing is not always better.

Carbohydrates (carbs) are found in:

- bread, pasta and noodles
- cereals
- some vegetables (like potatoes, sweet potatoes, peas and corn)
- legumes (beans, lentils, chickpeas)
- fruits and fruit juices
- milk and yoghurt
- all forms of sugar (sucrose, fructose, lactose and glucose, etc.)

Carbs are the body's main fuel supply and should be included in every meal and snack. Oils and fats can also fuel the body, but they are less effective and produce far more negative side effects, so they are far less desirable.

Meat and other forms of protein like tofu and soy are also essential, but they are not fuel for bodily functions. Their main role is to build cells and strengthen tissues.

Carbs break down in the body to form glucose, the fuel which powers our engine. Glucose is carried by the blood to all parts of the body. It is absorbed into the cells and burned to supply the energy for all bodily functions — including brain function.

Too many carbs (that is, too much food) means that there is more glucose in the bloodstream than the body can use. Being the efficient machine that it is, however, the body eventually converts excess glucose into fat and stores it for future use — for a time when food may not be in such abundant supply.

This survival mechanism has evolved over millions of years of famine and feast, and is a perfect adaptation for an uncertain environment. Unfortunately, as we no longer live in an uncertain environment, this fat-store is usually unnecessary, as we rarely experience famine in the modern world — at least, not in first-world societies.

A diet that is high in carbs, oils and fats, therefore, is one which will result in an increase in body weight. As 'fastfood' is a diet high in all these elements, and as the consumption of 'fastfood' is increasing — especially in the young — it is not difficult to understand the reason for what is being called 'the international obesity epidemic'.

> **Children, from a young age, are becoming overweight and obese in increasing numbers, and the future risk of heart attack, diabetes, stroke, asthma and other weight-related conditions is troubling — ESPECIALLY AS IT IS AN ENTIRELY AVOIDABLE 'EPIDEMIC'.**

What about G.I.?

In recent years, much has been written about the importance of a food's 'G.I.'. So, what exactly is G.I. and why is it so important?

G.I. stands for Glycaemic Index — another example of scientists using indecipherable words to express important, but not-so-complex ideas.

A food's Glycaemic Index measures how quickly it converts to glucose when it is digested. High G.I. foods break down quickly, while low G.I. foods break down more slowly.

So, high G.I. foods release glucose swiftly, and the blood glucose level rises rapidly. However, a sharp rise in blood glucose triggers the release of the hormone insulin, which accelerates the burning of blood glucose, so the level drops rapidly, leaving you feeling lethargic and in need of a further 'sugar-hit'.

This 'yo-yo' effect develops unhealthy eating habits. It is the reason that people with a high intake of sugars (in soft drinks and sweets, for example) are more likely to develop sugar cravings, and dangerous long-term dietary behaviours.

Low G.I. foods break down more slowly, and the effect is a more even release of glucose and less 'highs and lows'.

Look at these graphs:

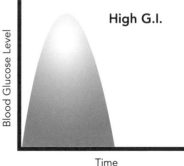

High G.I.

Blood Glucose Level

Time

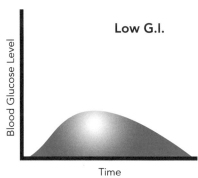

Low G.I.

Blood Glucose Level

Time

Excessive intake of high G.I. foods is seen as one cause of hyperactive behaviour and what teachers and early childhood carers sometimes refer to as the 'mid-afternoon blues', when children lose energy and sometimes 'drift off', as sugar levels plummet.

Carbohydrate-induced hyperactive behaviour should not be confused with ADHD (Attention Deficit Hyperactivity Disorder) — though a high G.I. intake can exacerbate the ADHD symptoms.

Of all carbohydrate sources, the simple sugars (sucrose, fructose, lactose and glucose are the most common) and highly processed flours (such as those found in white bread and hamburger buns) have the highest G.I. This means that soft drinks, candies, desserts and other high-sugar products, as well as white bread should only make up a small part of a child's daily intake.

On the other hand, mixed grain breads, oats, basmati rice, untoasted muesli, pasta and noodles, bran, most common fruits (except watermelon and canned lychees), legumes and milk products have the lowest G.I.

There is strong evidence that eating low G.I. foods can also have the effect of 'slowing down' the release of glucose from the higher G.I. foods in a child's diet.

> **So, be prepared.**
> **Planning your child's daily menu in advance —**
> **including low G.I. snacks — avoids the temptation**
> **to give in to the hype and buy a junk-food snack.**

How to Encourage Positive Food Choices

Children learn about nutrition primarily from their parents' example.

The eating habits established by parents tend to have a great influence on a child's future food choices. This is why it is so important to take control early, while your influence is strong.

> **Refusing to eat a particular food should not be seen**
> **as simple disobedience. It is an example of children**
> **demonstrating their growing independence and**
> **individuality. How we respond is key to whether the**

refusal ends up as a 'battle of wills' or an 'exercise in compromise'.

As most eating behaviours are based on habit, it is important not to reinforce the habit of refusal — as it will then become easier and easier for the child to refuse new tastes, and you can never win a food battle, as you cannot 'force-feed' your child without negative emotional consequences for you both.

Instead, compromise. Do not force the child to eat a particular food, but insist that the food remains on the plate throughout the meal (as many children will attempt to have it removed completely). Keep serving the food in small amounts, whether it is eaten or not, and use subtle encouragements from time to time, until you find an inducement that works.

One technique is to (without finishing your own portion) ask if you can have a little of the children's — being careful to leave some on their plate. This reinforces the 'desirability' of the food, without forcing the issue. Then casually ask if they would like to try some from your plate.

This is a game that adds new interest into the meal-time regime. The break in routine will often act as a 'circuit-breaker' in the refusal cycle, and induce the child to try the food. But don't then pounce and say, 'See, I told you you'd eat it!' This isn't about winning the point — it's about widening the child's tastes. Changing habits is a slow process, so be patient...

As children get older, their extended family, childcare providers and friends also influence their food choices. This is why parents, extended family and care-givers should work together to establish a commitment to healthy eating.

Establishing healthy eating habits in children requires commitment and consistency on the part of parents. Parents need to be clear about the nutritional messages they want to give their children, and can convey this with comments such as 'When you eat like this you will grow up big and strong', or 'Vegetables are so good for you'.

When children hear, see and experience the same messages over time, those messages naturally become very powerful.

Preparation and planning play a very important part in successfully establishing healthy eating habits in young children. When parents are organised and plan shopping and meals in advance they are more in control of what their children eat.

Outside food choices are rarely as nutritionally beneficial for children as home-cooked meals, and preventing a habit is always easier than breaking one. As with any other aspect of a child's life where a parent wishes to make a positive impact, prevention is better than cure.

Here are some suggestions to encourage your child to develop healthy eating habits:

- **Be a Role Model** — It is much easier to teach children to make healthy eating choices if you make the same choices.

  Modelling good eating habits has a powerful impact on children. When your child sees you snacking on apples instead of chocolate cake, she is far more likely to copy.

- **Eat Together as a Family** — Our lives and careers are increasingly busy, and to coordinate all family members to eat meals together can sometimes be a challenge. However, research has shown that families who eat together produce children who have healthy attitudes to food and make better food choices in their adulthood.[16]

- **Make Meal Times Happy** — Consider family meals to be pleasant social events that bring the family together to talk about the positive daily events and memories.

  Being relaxed and smiling is a great way to enjoy a meal. Avoid reprimanding or arguing whilst eating as this can lead to children developing negative attitudes to food.

- **Encourage Children to Try New Foods** — Children often have very simple tastes and can sometimes be reluctant to try new foods.

  If you are introducing a new food to your child, serve it in a small quantity, along with foods that the child really enjoys.

  Many pre-school-aged children are 'picky eaters', unwilling to taste unfamiliar foods. They can also be unpredictable in their food preferences. Some days they will say they love a particular food, even when the following day they will refuse to eat it.

Encourage a sense of adventure about food. Gradually introducing new foods can help overcome 'preference challenges'.

- **Avoid Using Food as a Reward or Punishment** — Many parents find it convenient to make the statement, '*If you eat your dinner you can have your dessert*', indicating that children will receive a reward (dessert) for doing something they do not really want to do (eat dinner).

  But consider the effect of this strategy for winning obedience. It is a strategy that places higher value on the dessert, which is the less healthy food. If you are offering a dessert, consider it as part of the balanced meal and not as a treat.

  It is not advisable to use favourite foods as a reward for good or compliant behaviour.

- **Provide Healthy Snacks** — Regularly scheduled snacks between meals can help regulate children's energy levels, sugar and moods, and keep them on a more 'even keel' throughout the day.

  Preparing healthy snacks such as diced fruit and vegetables, whole-grain biscuits and bread, yoghurt and cheese, in advance, can ensure that you avoid the need to purchase expensive unhealthy snacks.

- **Provide Choice** — It is always a good parenting strategy to provide children with the opportunity to make a choice between options. The trick is that parents can ensure that all options are good, and, in the case of food, it is fairly easy to ensure that all options are healthy food!

  An example of giving a child a choice of snack could be '*Would you like banana or apple for your snack today?*' rather than '*What would you like for your snack?*' (which opens up too many undesirable alternatives) or '*Would you like banana or a chocolate?*' (which is liable to result in the less healthy option).

> **Remember, the person asking the question controls the situation. So, make sure you ask the right question.**

Once children make a choice, it is rare that they go back on it. Giving them a choice of two acceptable alternatives is a strategy which works in many areas — not just with food.

Parents often complain that they have battles with their children at meal times, often where the child is refusing to eat certain foods or finish a meal. Here are some ideas we recommend that may reduce challenges at meal times:

- **Trust When Your Child is Full** — Children need to learn to understand when their bodies tell them they are full. This is an important lesson as they become able to regulate their food intake.

  However, we know that children learn to use the excuse 'I'm full', when they don't want to eat their meal as well, so it is a challenge for parents to tell the difference!

  That having been said, it is an old fashioned idea to insist that children eat everything that is on their plate. Research has shown that this practice is likely to lead to children compulsively overeating in the future.[17]

  We have to take into account when the child last ate, or if they are tired or unwell, as an indication of whether they are genuinely full or whether to insist on them eating some more.

  In general, children show us they are full when they start playing with their food.

- **Express Excitement about What You Are Eating** — Children do not like to miss out on something special. If you genuinely enjoy your food, make sure you express it verbally to your child, for example, '*This fish is sooo delicious. I just love it*'.

  It is vitally important that children learn to feel a sense of enjoyment about eating healthy food, and parents can do much to generate this positive feeling. Children will be more inclined to eat the food they have found past enjoyment in eating.[18]

  This way, your children may also consider that what you are eating is special, and they will want to join in.

- **Notice When Your Child is Trying Something New or Eating Well** — Children love attention, and they will even seek negative attention if they have to. Unfortunately, meal times can be an opportunity for children to gain negative attention, such as, '*Eat your food, NOW!*'

  This is where parents can modify their behaviour to 'catch their child doing something good' instead. Without making too much fuss, parents can casually comment if their child has tried a new food or is eating well, for example, 'You are eating so well today. What a great eater', accompanied by a smile. Noticing when your child is doing well is a great motivator and can be very powerful.

As parents, we also want our children to develop a positive attitude toward food and become knowledgeable enough about it to be able to make informed choices. Here are some suggestions to help your child develop a general awareness and appreciation of food:

- **Talk about Food Enthusiastically** — A parent's attitude to food has a big impact on their children. If a parent has knowledge about food, combinations of flavours and nutritional content of food this can provide some very interesting conversation for children. For example, a parent might say, 'Did you know that vegetables with dark green leaves help the cells in your body to repair themselves? This means that if you fall over and scrape your knee, eating green vegetables will make your knee get better much quicker!'

- **Involve Children in Weekly Meal Plans** — When children feel that they are involved in a decision, they are more likely to cooperate with their parents.

  For example, if children are given a choice about which days of the week they would like certain meals, they may be more willing to eat the food given. This is why making a weekly meal plan with children is a good idea.

  If you ask your child which day of the week s/he would like to eat pasta, then write on a calendar the day the child chooses. You can create a 'build-up' to the meal, and the child will look forward to it with anticipation.

- **Allow Children to Make Simple Recipes** — Under adult supervision, young children are very capable of making simple foods.

  For example, if a parent cuts vegetables into small pieces children can be inventive and use toothpicks to make 'vegetable people' — or likewise, with fruit, children can easily make a fruit salad, or fruit kebabs.

  When children engage in cooking, food preparation and tasting/ sampling, you give them the opportunity to experiment with food through their senses. This engages them enthusiastically about food.[19]

  Another example would be to make whole-grain muffins with your child, allowing them to add and mix the ingredients. There are children's recipe books available that use pictures as the instructions.[20]

- **Take Your Child to a Farm** — Children who live in the city can sometimes believe that food just comes from a supermarket or local market.

    Taking children to a working farm will give them an experiential understanding of where fruits and vegetables come from and how they are grown. This knowledge can increase a child's appreciation and enthusiasm about food. Parents could even grow some vegetables or herbs in pots at home.

While it is important for parents to be committed to healthy food for their children, it is equally important not to convey any anxiety about food. When parents become anxious about food, children can pick up on this and may develop negative attitudes towards eating.

Be reassured that nutrition is not a problem for children if they are growing, active and look healthy. Planning is the key to the successful implementation of our healthy eating recommendations. Begin by keeping only healthy foods in your home, and planning meals to avoid fastfood options. Modelling healthy habits, preparing meals together and enjoying happy family meals can have children well on the way to being healthy eaters in childhood and as adults.

To Do...

1. Fill in the 'Examples' section with the types of foods from each Food Group you offer your children each day.

Food Group	Recommnended Daily Servings	Examples
Grains — Bread, Cereal, Rice, Pasta	6	
Vegetables	5	
Fruit	3	
Dairy — Milk, Yoghurt, Cheese	2	
Protein — Meat, Poultry, Fish, Dry Beans, Eggs	2	
Fats, Oils, Sweets	Use Sparingly	

To Do...

2. Make a daily meal plan for your child with two to three variations for each meal. Cross check your meal plan with the daily requirements of each food group.

Breakfast	Option 1
	Option 2
	Option 3
Morning Snack	Option 1
	Option 2
	Option 3
Lunch	Option 1
	Option 2
	Option 3
Afternoon Snack	Option 1
	Option 2
	Option 3
Dinner	Option 1
	Option 2
	Option 3

3. Below we have created a 'sample meal plan' as a guide for planning meals and snacks for your pre-school child. We encourage you to adapt it to suit personal and cultural food preferences. If you replace an item, make sure that it is with another food from that food group to keep your child's diet balanced.

MEAL	MON	TUES	WED
B'FAST	• Whole-wheat/ multi-grain toast • Canned fruit • Milk	• Grain cereal like weetbix • Orange slices • Milk	• Porridge • Apple slices • Milk
SNACK	• Banana • Cheese • Whole-wheat crackers • Water	• Wholemeal roll • Cheese • Orange juice	• Apple • Milkshake • Blueberry wholemeal muffin
LUNCH	• Chicken • Shredded lettuce • Tomato pita wrap • Apple slices • Milk	• Tuna sandwich • Raw carrot and celery with Hummus dip • Milk	• Pasta and cheese • Steamed carrot, zucchini and broccoli • Whole-grain and sultana biscuit • Milk
SNACK	• Blueberry muffin • Apple or orange juice	• Water • Crackers • Tub diced fruit	• Whole-wheat crackers • Apple slices • Water
SUPPER	• Lamb chop • Potatoes with steamed vegetables • Tub diced fruit • Whole-grain biscuit • Milk	• Minced beef burger pattie in whole-grain bun, lettuce • Chips • Frozen yoghurt • Water	• Tuna pasta baked with cheese and steamed vegetables • Tub diced fruit • Milk

THURS	FRI	SAT	SUNDAY
• Crumpet with cheese • Orange or apple juice • Milk	• Grain cereal like Weetbix • Fresh or dried fruit • Milk	• Pancakes • Fresh or frozen berries • Syrup • Milk	• Scrambled or poached eggs • Whole-wheat/multi-grain toast and jam • Apple juice
• Banana • Cheese on whole-wheat crackers • Water	• Milkshake • Orange • Whole-wheat crackers • Water	• Apple • Tub yoghurt • Wholemeal crackers • Milk	• Banana • Wholemeal muffin • Milk
• Vegetable soup • Hummus dip and pita bread • Tub yoghurt • Water	• Pumpkin • Whole-grain muffin • Frozen yoghurt • Milk	• Ham cheese tomato sandwich • Melon slices • Milk	• Beef shredded lettuce carrot pita wrap • Oatmeal cookies • Milk
• Fruit • Yoghurt • Water	• Apple • Muffin • Water	• Raw carrot and celery Hummus dip • Water	• Banana • Whole-wheat muffin • Milk
• Roast chicken with steamed vegetables • Whole-wheat bread • Milk	• Lamb kebabs with steamed green vegetables • Frozen yoghurt • Water	• Crumbed fish with steamed vegetables • Banana muffin • Milk	• Chicken pasta with tomato sauce • Steamed green vegetables • Ice cream • Water

C: The Many Benefits of Laughter

Giggles that Make the 'Grey Matter' Grow!

> **Seven days without laughter makes one weak.**
> **— Mort Walker**

Everybody loves to laugh — it is, without question, one of the great gifts that life has to offer us, in an often-much-too-serious world.

There is, however, a good deal of unnecessary disagreement about when laughter is appropriate and when it isn't — even for young children.

Laughter generally has the stigma of being appropriate only in relaxed social situations. There is a general unstated consensus that the activities of work and learning should be more serious endeavours.

It may surprise you to learn that, in fact, laughter actually promotes thinking and problem-solving at a higher level. It makes you healthier and happier, and it actually grows connections within your brain![21]

In terms of brain research, laughter has a serious scientific side. Research conducted over the past 30 years or so demonstrates that, for human beings, the mere act of laughing has many physiological, neurological, cognitive and psychological benefits.

Laughter and Learning

Renowned psychologist and philosopher, Dr Jean Houston, once wrote:

> **At the height of laughter, the universe is flung into a kaleidoscope of new possibilities.**

Recent brain research has discovered that laughter can be a very powerful ingredient in the learning process. In formal learning situations, it may appear that laughter is just children being silly, but laughter actually enables better connectivity between the brain's neurons — which helps children learn more quickly and store information more permanently.

From a psycho-behavioural perspective, this phenomenon is related to neural patterning and how the brain lays down information.

All learning passes through the limbic system (the emotions), before it is distributed to the rest of the brain. This means that the emotion we are experiencing at the time we learn something is stored, along with the learning, when we lay down long-term memories — and when, at some later stage, we recall that piece of learning, the emotional resonance stored with it also resurfaces.

If I associate a particular learning with a negative emotion (like fear, anxiety, confusion, boredom or frustration, for example), I am, as a consequence, reluctant to access and use that information. This is because, subconsciously, I do not wish to relive that negative emotion.

This avoidance is an example of what psychologists call 'negative reinforcement' — not doing something in order to avoid repeating a negative emotional experience.

It is the source, in older children and teens, of statements like 'I hate maths/English/history'. They do not 'hate' the subject. Rather, it is an attempt to avoid the negative emotions associated with the learning, and the resistance translates to an inability to perform — creating further discomfort and reluctance — a negative emotional cycle that can affect their future learning success.

It is a cycle that, sadly, often has its roots in a child's pre-school learning experiences.

> ## Laughter, on the other hand, is one of the most positive experiences in life.

Any information or learning associated with an emotional state that produces laughter will produce a 'positive reinforcement' — repeating a behaviour in order to re-experience a positive emotion.

Associating laughter with learning encourages a 'positive learning cycle' and a positive long-term relationship with learning.

Watch babies and young children sharing an activity which makes them laugh.

They are quite capable of repeating the same action or pattern of behaviour for as long as it elicits a laugh. And remember, for young children, repetition of this sort (not boring rote repetition, but fun repetitive behaviour) is the way that learning is cemented in the neural networks — the foundation 'root-system' — of the brain.

Laughter also makes learning more enjoyable — and if learning is more enjoyable, children are more likely to want to learn!

According to Dr William Fry, Professor Emeritus at Stanford Medical School:

Laughter aids memory and increases alertness and concentration.

Laughter, fun and humour serve an important developmental function for young children, as a way to express their growing powers of reasoning and creativity. The educational value of this bond between laughter and learning is inestimable.[22]

With laughter as an element in the learning process, children will learn and retain more of what you teach them, and you will both enjoy every minute of it.

The Physiological Benefits of Laughter

When a person laughs, carbon dioxide leaves the body and is replaced by oxygen-rich air. This stimulates the production of anti-inflammatory agents, encourages muscles to relax and oxygenates muscles and other tissues all over the body, from the scalp to the legs, all the while reducing levels of the stress hormone *cortisol*.[23]

The physiological study of laughter is called 'gelotology' (from the Greek 'gelos'/'gelotos' — meaning laughter).

Gelotology reveals that laughter seems to be produced via a circuit that runs through many regions of the brain. Three main areas of the brain that are activated during laughter are:

1. **The cognitive (thinking) regions of the brain** — which help you 'get' a joke. This includes parts of the frontal lobe near the forehead — a key area for future logical thinking and decision-making.

2. **The motor regions of the brain** — which help move the muscles of the face to smile and laugh.

3. **The emotional regions of the brain** — which help produce the happy feelings that accompany a cheerful experience.[24]

The Health Benefits of Laughter

Just a few fun experiences a week will elevate serotonin levels and help boost your immune system and improve your health — and, by extension, your longevity (life expectancy).

> ## A Science Fact:
> **Serotonin is a neurotransmitter, sometimes known as the 'feel-good' chemical. It has a powerful effect on mood and anxiety, and is associated with feelings of serenity and optimism.**
>
> **Serotonin also has significant positive effects on other key areas — including sleep, appetite, pain relief and blood pressure.**

Increasingly, studies are demonstrating that laughter and humour boost immunity, diminish pain, and help people deal with the stress of life.[25]

Incongruity and Laughter — Humour as Training for Creative Thinking

Children enjoy incongruity.

Incongruity means something that is out of place, implausible or absurd — a logical or causal disconnect — such as a cat wearing a hat, or mum wearing a moustache. Both these occurrences would cause laughter in pre-school children.

Children love incongruity in language, particularly the stringing together of rhyming words or nonsense syllables. Because language is supposed to be logical and orderly, and sentences don't usually rhyme, it seems funny to children when the usual 'rules' don't seem to apply.

> **Almost anything that goes against what children consider normal and predictable can make them laugh.**

Children also like to push the boundaries of what is considered socially acceptable, just to see how far they can be pushed. This is why 'bathroom humour' is popular with pre-schoolers.

Pre-schoolers know that certain words are unacceptable and they may try to use them deliberately for shock value. Often the expression on a parent's face is the source of much laughter and entertainment for young children.

So, how does this love of incongruity help children develop their learning and thinking skills?

Learning is, by its very nature, an alteration of the status quo — a change in the universe of what was previously known. The new world created by new knowledge, is, therefore, incongruous, with the old one to a greater or lesser extent. Humour helps children prepare for this reality, by making such 'disconnects' fun — and nothing to be disturbed by.

Similarly, creativity — like humour — involves making novel and previously un-thought-of connections in response to a given problem or a goal.

> **A child who enjoys humour — who looks for the fun in the 'creative disconnect' — is a creative adult in training.**

'Silliness' — a Building Block of Social Skills, Cognition and Creativity

Young children have a special preference for silliness. Experts believe that silliness has important developmental benefits for building social skills, cognitive thinking and creativity. Laughter creates a bond between people. As children grow and their social world expands, they will use the link of silliness and laughter to solidify other friendships.

Stretching the imagination, thinking outside the box, and learning to look at a situation from different angles are other long-term benefits of developing a sense of humour.

Child psychologist Niki Saros observes that children who are creative thinkers have a certain mental flexibility that allows them to escape from the pressures of a 'hyper-structured' view of the world.

Humour develops that flexibility, and that skill translates to creative problem-solving down the road. Research conducted by creativity experts E Paul Torrance and T Wu[26] into indicators of creativity in children, have shown that children who are creative thinkers — those willing to think 'outside the box' (a key element of humour) — tend to be the ones who produce the most creative and original ideas as adults.

How to Make Your Child Laugh at Any Age

Christine Puder, in her article *The Healthful Effects of Laughter*[27] (based on the research of McGhee[28]) summarises the development stages of children's humour. This is a helpful reference for any parent keen to make their children laugh at any age!

The following are some of the key developmental stages in your child's sense of humour.

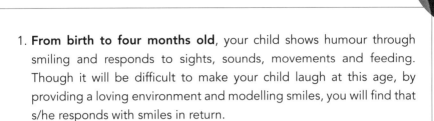

1. **From birth to four months old**, your child shows humour through smiling and responds to sights, sounds, movements and feeding. Though it will be difficult to make your child laugh at this age, by providing a loving environment and modelling smiles, you will find that s/he responds with smiles in return.

2. **From four months to eight months**, laughter can be generated at physical level through active stimulation. At this stage children are discovering body movements, recognising human faces and voices, and you can make them laugh with physical contact games like *'I'm gonna get you!'* or *'Here it comes!'* or by just tickling them.

3. **Eight months to one year** sees your child laughing when in contact with toys. This is also the time when s/he is beginning to distinguish between self and non-self, and is amused by incongruity (the inconsistent behaviour of people or objects). It is the stage where peek-a-boo and simple magic tricks (making a ball appear or disappear) can evoke a strong laughter response.

4. **From one to two years**, incongruent behaviour, repetitive behaviour or expectancy violations (unexpected results) will become the primary source of laughter, as the child is developing organised schemas of the world. At this stage, you can make your child laugh by mislabelling objects and people — that is, calling them by the wrong names. It is also the time when playing with toys in an unusual way (making it tow-truck bark, or the dog say meow) will seem incredibly funny.

5. **From two to six years**, fantasy, make-believe, slapstick, silly words and songs, and bodily noises all become sources of mirth. It is important at this age that the child be directly involved in the humorous activity. This is the time when active play and the sound of words — such as the nonsense words in Dr Seuss, or simple funny songs — become a favourite source of humour.

Language Games to Make Children Laugh

The following short games can be played at any time: during dinner, in the car or as a little break in homework for older children. Whilst these games are silly and fun, they also teach children important concepts and rules about language and grammar.

(a) Gobbledegook — Meaning Mayhem!

Gobbledegook is a nonsense language. It's a string of sounds that have form, but no meaning, so the meaning has to be expressed through vocal intonation and body language. It may contain some linking words which children can recognise — this makes it easier for them to join in and make up their own gobbledegook — but most of the key meaning words (verbs, nouns, adverbs and adjectives, etc.) should be nonsense.

> Examples of gobbledegook might be:
> *'The slithy bandersnatch gribbled in the storch. Krebble him!'*
> *'Gremble me! I want to schmooch you!'*
> *'Trickle your plomb and grind over here! The mistlesnacker is coming!'*

1. Ask a question in gobbledegook. The response can be a shake of the head either 'yes' or 'no' or more gobbledegook!

2. Encourage conversation in gobbledegook.

3. Young children love to play this game. They can make up any sounds that they wish as they talk in gobbledegook.

(b) Name Nonsense — Rhymes that Rock!

1. Make up a rhyme based on the names of people you know. Even if the rhyming word doesn't make sense, listening to the rhyme will be fun.

2. Use this verse form for each name:

What's your name?
My name is Fred.
Fred, Fred, spends all day in bed.

What's your name?
My name is Irene.
Irene, Irene, should be heard, but never seen.

What's your name?
My name is Brian.
Brian, Brian is always cryin'.

Many more 'laughter inducing games' can be found in *The Learning Power of Laughter* by Jackie Silberg.[29]

Practising the Gift

Because so much learning power exists in a good laugh, it is important to use this wonderful gift frequently.

The multiple benefits of laughter — physiological, neurological, cognitive and psychological — build a strong case for developing a great sense of humour in your family.

Share your laughter and help make others laugh. Share your humorous perspective and give others permission to do the same. Tell jokes around the dinner table.

A good sense of humour is something everyone can work on. Applying laughter to learning will not only make your child's learning journey more fun, it will also help them to learn faster and more permanently — and allow them to enjoy happy academic success!

To Do...

1. Try the two language activities described earlier. Enjoy the giggles and laughter they generate in your family.

2. Think about these questions:

   a. What has been your opinion of laughter and learning in the past?

   b. After reading the material presented in this section, has your opinion:

      a) stayed the same;

      b) shifted slightly; or

      c) completely changed?

   c. What challenges might there be to managing laughter during learning?

   d. How can parents and teachers 'strike a balance' in relation to learning and laughter?

D: Getting Your Child Moving

The Importance of Exercise in Early Childhood

> **Gardens are not made by sitting in the shade.**
> **— Rudyard Kipling**

Do your pre-schooler a favour. Turn off the TV — say goodbye to the purple dinosaur, the hairy puppets and the talking yellow sponge — and step outside for a game of catch or hide-and-seek.

Or, better still, share a short visit to the local playground — and this time, join in the fun, instead of sitting in the shade reading that magazine, or checking emails on your Blackberry.

According to the World Health Organisation,[30] regular exercise builds endurance and muscle strength; it improves bone health; it lowers risk factors for serious health problems like heart disease, colon cancer and diabetes in later life; it keeps blood pressure in check and, just as importantly, it fosters self-esteem.

Oh, and it's good for the kids, too!

First, the Science

In the area of exercise and cognition, science once again has something to teach the parents of today's pre-schoolers. A rapidly-growing body of research indicates that *cognitive growth and learning are actually stimulated by physical movement.*[31]

> **If you want to find out more about this important relationship and other benefits of physical activity in young children, we have included some further reading in the Bibliography at the end of the book.**

The research not only highlights the obvious fact that the brain and body are connected, but it also demonstrates the truth of a common-sense assumption that they are interdependent — that what happens in the body affects the brain.[32]

> **All children need a healthy body to house a healthy brain.**

At the 2007 *Society for Neuroscience* Conference, no less than 80 studies suggested strong links between the cerebellum (the brain's movement centre) and memory, spatial perception, language, attention, emotion, non-verbal cues and decision-making.

Studies in neuro-psychology also support the view that learning and motor development are closely related. They suggest that the brain regions that control cognitive and motor functions are often activated together. In fact, research findings strongly indicate that exercise and mental activity actually generate and sustain more brain cells.[33]

This is particularly true of the pre-frontal cortex (the part of the brain directly behind the forehead), which is vital for complex cognitive tasks, and the cerebellum (at the base of the brain), which is important in controlling motor skills. Research shows that the two are often co-activated.

Children engaged in daily physical education show superior motor fitness and academic performance, and research suggests that physical exercise boosts brain function, improves mood and increases learning.

This may be because people who exercise produce more neural connections, and also because exercise increases the flow of blood — and, therefore, oxygen — to the brain.

The theories of renowned developmental psychologist Jean Piaget centred around the link between increasing physical mastery and cognitive development. He found that developments in motor skills also influence cognitive development. Subsequent research found that crawlers perform better than pre-crawlers of the same age on Piaget's A-not-B task.[34]

Early childhood is a critical time for both sides of the brain to be developed in tandem, because of the 'cross-referencing' that occurs during this period of life. Physical exercise which works both sides of the brain simultaneously strengthens the connections between the two hemispheres of the brain. When children are engaged in creative movement, they are involved in activities that will increase their memory and their ability to communicate.

Guidelines

Early Childhood Guidelines for the minimum-required physical activity for pre-schoolers — in the USA, Australia and Singapore — show that children need at least 30 to 60 minutes of developmentally appropriate structured physical activity of a moderate to vigorous nature every day.

The American Heart Association and The National Association for Sports and Physical Education (NASPE) both recommend that toddlers get at least 30 minutes of structured physical activity each day and that pre-schoolers get at least 60.

In addition, all children should get between 60 minutes and several hours per day of unstructured activity. Toddlers and pre-schoolers shouldn't be physically inactive (except, of course, while sleeping) for more than 60 minutes at a time.

Pre-schoolers develop important motor skills as they grow. New skills your pre-schooler may be showing off include:

- hopping
- jumping forward
- catching a ball
- doing a somersault
- skipping
- balancing on one foot

Aerobic exercises (like running, jumping and chasing a ball) help develop your child's cardiovascular fitness. Strength and flexibility exercises (like climbing and stretching) help your child develop strong bones and muscles and improve your child's balance and coordination.

The American Academy of Pediatrics recommends that free play should be the first focus of any physical activity. Free play that is carefully planned to provide chances for pre-schoolers to acquire and fine-tune basic motor skills and to reach their capacity at their own speed, is better than structured play for pre-schoolers.

What Is Structured Play?

Pre-schoolers are likely to get structured play at childcare or in pre-school programmes through games like 'Duck, Duck, Goose' and 'London Bridge'.

Your pre-schooler can get structured outdoor play at home, too. Play together in the backyard or practice motor skills, such as throwing and catching a ball. Pre-schoolers also love trips to the playground.

Though many kids tend to gravitate toward the outdoors, lots of fun physical activities can be organised indoors, too:

- a child-friendly indoor obstacle course

- a treasure hunt
- forts made out of sheets and boxes or chairs

Designate a play area and clear the space of any breakables.

Many parents are eager to enrol their pre-school child in organised sports. Although some leagues may be open to children as young as four years old, organised and team sports are not recommended until a child is a little older. Pre-schoolers can't understand complex rules and often lack the attention span, skills and coordination needed to play sports.

If your pre-schoolers are not ready for the team or not interested in sports, consider focussing instead on helping them continue to work on fundamental skills — hopping on one foot, catching a ball, doing a somersault, and maybe riding a bicycle or tricycle.

Below, are a few exercises for you to try at home.

For more structured play activities, see Volume Two Chapter Eight: *Play is Not a Four-Letter Word*.

To Do...

Help your child to stay active by exercising together!

Moderate to Vigorous Structured Lounge-Room Exercises for Toddlers and Their Parents:

1. **Walking the Tightrope**
   Purpose: Helps develop balance. Exercises foot muscles.
   a) Place a piece of masking tape on the floor.
   b) Walk together along the 'tightrope'.
   c) Try to stay on the line. Walk backwards, forwards and sideways. Try 'bunny-hopping' or hopping on one leg.

2. **Treasure Hunt**
   Purpose: Exercises gross and fine motor skills. Helps develop memory skills.
   a) Hide an item or items such as, toys, shapes around the room or yard,
   b) Ask your child to move around to find the missing item/s in various ways, such as crawling, walking, jumping, or slithering like a snake.

3. **Songs and Movement, such as:**
   'Head, shoulders, knees and toes'
   Purpose: Helps your child identify body parts. Also helps with flexibility and understanding the concepts of up, down, low and high.
   a) Stand facing your child.
   b) Slowly call out the names of each body part in the title, asking your child to touch.

4. **Jump and Twist**
   Purpose: Strengthens legs and improves circulation.
   a) Hold your child's hands as you jump together as high as you can.
   b) Put as much spring into your jump as possible. Land with ankles and knees slightly bent.
   c) Then jump with hands by your sides.
   d) Twist feet and hips and pump arms from side to side.

5. **Rock and Roll**
   Purpose: Stretches back and strengthens abdominal muscles.
   a) Sit on the floor and clasp your hands under your knees. Tell your child to do what you do.
   b) Rock on your back and keep your hands tucked.
   c) Don't rock on your shoulders — it will strain your neck and make rocking difficult.
   d) After several repetitions, alternate with side-to-side rocking.

6. **The Mirror Game**
   Purpose: Good for coordination — children must repeat what they see. Also provides flexibility and aerobic activity.
   a) Tell your children to do exactly as you do, as if they were your reflection in the mirror.
   b) Make slow movements. Take turns being the leader.
   c) Make movements that require flexibility and exercise. Bend at the waist, stretch your hands overhead, stand on tiptoes, do deep knee bends, run in place, etc.

E: The Importance of the 'D' Factor

The 'Dark Side of Tanning' — the Bright Side of U-V Radiation

> **No ray of sunshine is ever lost.**
> **— Albert Schweitzer**

Life is about balance — and nowhere is this truer than in the area of sunlight exposure.

In recent years, our understanding of the dangers associated with excessive exposure to ultra-violet radiation (UVR) and its link to melanoma (skin cancer), has increased significantly. This danger is particularly strong in Australia, whose harsh sun and environmental conditions have earned it the dubious title of 'the world's skin cancer capital', with twice the melanoma rate of any other country.

The *Dark Side of Tanning* website, which is a project of the NSW government in Australia, and the Cancer Institute, NSW, has this to say about sun exposure:

> **Sun exposure causes damage to your skin which accumulates over your lifetime and can lead to skin cancer. Because damage adds up, it's important to protect your skin whatever your age.**

This means beginning when a child is very young.

The publicity relating to 'sun-safe' behaviour stresses protection in the form of protective clothing, sunscreens and blockouts, the wearing of hats — and, of course, staying out of the sun when it is at its hottest in late morning and early afternoon.

This is very sensible advice — even in countries where the sun is not so punishing. The 'downside' of this growing awareness, however, is that some parents, especially those of very young children, can sometimes over-react to the threat posed by the sun, by keeping them indoors and avoiding exposure of any kind.

This approach is counter-productive, as the human body is genetically programmed to respond to sunlight, and without any exposure, it cannot function effectively.

Recent research is forcing us to refine our sun-exposure policy — particularly for vulnerable groups including infants and young children. In fact, an April 2008 *Environmental Health Perspectives* report shows that avoiding the sun completely may be just as damaging to their health as over-exposure.

The good news is that there is no need to over-expose to reap the benefits of UVR. Even five to ten minutes' exposure per day on 40% of your child's skin surface can be enough to ensure good health.

Not to mention feeling a whole lot happier!

Why Is It So?

From your own experience, you know that being outside in the sun makes you feel good — and, in small 'doses', it really is good for your health!

After days of rain, or a cold winter, or even if you have been forced to stay indoors for an extended length of time, just standing outside and turning your face to the sun makes you feel so much better.

This is because the sunlight triggers an increase in the feel-good brain chemical serotonin. We have already seen (in *The Health Benefits of Laughter*) how serotonin lifts your mood and wards off depression, as well as controlling sleep patterns and other bodily functions.

The feel-good effects of sunlight start in the brain. When light enters your eyes, it not only goes to your visual cortex enabling you to see, it also goes to a part of the limbic system known as the hypothalamus. The hypothalamus controls body temperature, hunger and thirst, water balance and blood pressure. It links the nervous system to the endocrine system and controls the body's circadian rhythms (see *How Much Sleep Does My Child Need?*).

So, anything — like an inadequate exposure to sunlight — that disrupts these rhythms can significantly affect our body's ability to function properly.

The 'D' Factor

Sunlight also triggers the production of vitamin D, which is crucial to health. It regulates at least 1,000 different genes that affect the performance of virtually every tissue in the body.

Vitamin D not only builds strong bones and healthy teeth, but it also keeps the immune system working. Studies have shown that exposing the body to sunlight increases the number of white cells in the blood.

White cells are the body's first line of defence against infections and are key to your immune system's effective response to the bacteria, viruses and other organisms that cause illness. But it is not just germs that are a threat.

Cedric F Garland, a medical professor at the University of California, San Diego, suggests that maintaining the correct levels of vitamin D in the bloodstream long-term, reduces the risk of all forms of cancer — especially breast cancer.

> **Garland calls this 'the single most important action that could be taken by society to reduce the incidence of cancer... beyond not smoking.**

Vitamin D also increases the amount of oxygen that the blood transports around the body — and a higher concentration of oxygen increases energy, sharpens mental processes and makes you feel a whole lot better.

Although a small amount of vitamin D is obtained through a diet of cereals, fish and eggs, over 90% of the body's vitamin D requirement is produced simply by the effect of sunlight on the skin.

No wonder you feel better in the sun!

> **Vitamin D supplements are not the best answer for children (or adults!), because too many vitamin D supplements can be toxic in high doses — and it is too easy to overdose when using pills and capsules.**

Besides, the natural way is so much cheaper and easier — and more enjoyable!

Of course, if we are to take advantage of this 'bright side' of UVR exposure, we must use sunscreens and all other recommended measures to protect our child's delicate skin from damage — which may not show up in the form of cancerous changes for decades.

Still, as long as we follow these sensible precautions, we can achieve the all-important balance.

For more advice on skin protection, visit the *Dark Side of Tanning* website.[35] Its advice is very simple and easy to follow.

Playing It Safe

In a society that increasingly spends time indoors, make it a priority for your family to get outside every day — even on cloudy days, as the sun's UV rays penetrate clouds. If you know you'll be out for more than eight to ten minutes, play it safe and use protection.

Barbara A Gilchrest of Boston University School of Medicine points out that, according to the research, some sunlight enters the skin even through a high-SPF sunscreen, so people can maximise their dermal vitamin D production by spending additional time outdoors while wearing protection.

'Without the sunscreen,' she says, 'this same individual would be incurring substantially more damage to the skin but not further increasing the vitamin D level.'

Our greatest glory lies, not in never falling,
but in rising every time we fall.

Confucius

CHAPTER THREE

THE EMOTIONAL NEEDS

The Power of Mindset

(Building a Healthy and Resilient Self-Image in Your Child)

ADDIE

'…but the Queen just laughed, then her gaze went cold. "Forty days," she said. "And not one single minute more." And with those words, she closed the door of the tower-room, leaving poor Imogen with no choice.'

Adelaide pauses, hoping that closed lids mean sleep, but Imogen opens her eyes and smiles.

'I'm not asleep, Addie. Go on.'

'Where was I?'

'Leaving poor Imogen with no choice…' the child prompts, and it is Addie's turn to smile. The imitation of her 'narrator's tone' is a little too close to the mark.

'Right…' A deep breath. Imogen's eyes are fixed on the performance, now. Addie slips back into character. "Oh, how can I weave a portrait fit for a queen, with only spider silk and moonbeams?" cried the little princess. "What am I to do?"

'Then a tiny voice spoke from the mouse-hole in the wall.

' "Colour it with the brown from your hair, and the egg-shell blue from your eyes," it said.

' "Who's there?" cried Imogen, scared by the sudden words. But the voice continued.

' "Colour it with red from the blood of your finger, pierced by the silver needle as it flies and pink from the bloom of your cheeks."

' "Show yourself!" demanded Imogen, but the voice went on.

' "Adorn it with gold from your innocent heart and crystal from the tears which bead like diamonds upon your tender face. The colours of your sorrow will save your life."

' "Who are you?" Imogen asked again, but the voice had ceased to speak. She stared in silence at the tiny hole, but no words came.

'So, for forty days and thirty-nine nights, she laboured, weaving her tapestry from the silk of spiders' webs and the silver of moonlight, and colouring it with the brown from her hair, and the blue from her eyes and the red from the drops of precious blood that flowed when the needle pricked.

'And finally, it was finished. And it was perfect. On the fortieth evening, when the bolt slid open on the outside of the door, she was ready.

'As the Queen entered to look upon the result, she gazed at the delicate beauty and the exquisite colours of the embroidery, and knew that she had the most perfect portrait in the kingdom.

'But her joy was shortlived. For as she reached out to touch the perfect skin of the face in the tapestry, her fingers felt suddenly colder than a winter lake, and the chill spread slowly along her arm and deep into her chest. Then, as she turned her head to look at the girl to whom she had been so terribly cruel, her entire body turned to ice.

'And the look which froze forever upon her face was one of shock and fear. For before her blank stare, Imogen stood there more beautiful than ever — though her hair was snow-white, her eyes had lost their egg-shell blue, and her skin was like fine china; perfect and almost transparent. For she had spent all her colours on the tapestry, and there were none left for her to wear.

'And when the little princess made her way down into the town, the citizens gathered to stare at her passing, for they had never seen a more beautiful girl.'

As the story ends, there is silence.

In the hallway outside the bedroom door, Addie can see the 'Wall of Fame' — photographs of Imogen's family; formal poses and candid shots. And central to each picture, the pale, smiling face of the young girl who now lies in the bed beside her, her hair stark white, her eyes almost clear, her skin the delicate translucent pink of her condition.

She runs gentle fingers through the fine down of the child's hair.

'And I, my little princess, have never seen a more beautiful girl than you… Sleep time.'

'Who was in the hole?'

'The hole?'

'The voice. Who told her what to do?'

Addie shakes her head.

'Never miss a trick, do you?'

Imogen wrinkles her nose and shakes her head. 'Well?'

Addie looks around the room. Mr Smith is sitting on his haunches, next to the exercise wheel in his tiny cage. His naked tail curls through the wire, like a tiny segmented earthworm, and his pink eyes stare unblinking at them, as if he too has been listening to the story.

'A little white mouse.' Addie replies finally. 'Like Mr Smith over there.'

'Mr Smith is a rat.' Imogen sounds almost condescending. 'And he can't talk.'

'How do you know, Miss Smartypants?' Addie fusses with the blanket, drawing it up to Imogen's chin, flicking the girl's nose playfully with the tip of her index finger. 'Just because he doesn't speak to you. I was talking with him just yesterday, and he told me that every night, after you go to sleep —'

'I love you, Addie,' Imogen says, tired of the game. 'You're my first best friend.'

Leaning down to kiss her, Addie places her head on the pillow next to the child's pale skin, and whispers in her ear.

'And I love you, princess. Now go to sleep, or your parents won't be at all impressed when they get home.'

At the door, she stops to look back. Imogen has turned towards the wall, with her knees drawn up in foetal position under the covers.

"Night, Baby.'

'Leave the light on in the hall?' the little girl murmurs, but she is already asleep.

Addie hesitates, surveying the room one last time.

From his cage, Mr Smith stares back at her. His tail flicks lazily, and his whiskers catch the light from the hallway.

...with the brown from your hair, and the egg-shell blue from your eyes...?

Shut up, you! She throws the thought towards him. You couldn't do any better...

Imogen's Story

A babysitter is one part teacher, one part confidante and one part policeman, and at times she was each of those things, but for Addie there was another key element to the job description.

Story teller.

I lived for the moments when she would sit beside me on the bed, pulling the covers up to my neck, and ask, 'Where would you like to go tonight?' Or those times when she would take a deep breath, put on her 'storyteller's face', change her voice and announce, 'It's once-upon-a-time time. Are you ready?'

Does a fish breathe water?

And the story would begin.

She had a gift. I realise that now, in a way I couldn't have put into words back then. But though I didn't have the words, I think I knew.

That she was a genius, that the fire of imagination burned white-hot in her.

That her words were... golden.

I was six, and Addie came into my life like a change of seasons, magically transforming my 'difference' into something special. Something miraculous.

Her stories took me into worlds where a lack of pigmentation was no longer a curse that made you different. Where people stared at you, not because you were a freak of nature, but because of the amazing translucent beauty of your porcelain skin and the snowy perfection of your hair.

They changed the way I looked at myself...

This extract is from *Dream-Weaver* (one of Brian's short stories). It introduces us to Adelaide (Addie) and Imogen — and the special relationship they share.

So, why have we included it here?

This chapter is about transformation — about the difference a positive mindset and self-confidence can make, to the way a young child approaches the very real challenges of growing up strong and resilient.

And the story of Addie and Imogen is an ideal starting point for what will follow.

Who are Addie and Imogen, and what does their story have to do with our ability to prepare our children for life beyond the safe haven of the home? To answer this question, it is probably a good idea to look at the extract more closely.

Dream-Weaver is, in part, a story about the power of story, about its ability to shift our perspective, allowing us to see ourselves — and the world — in a different light. In *Volume Two*, we will look in greater detail at the importance of storytelling — and the art of engagement — in the life of a pre-schooler. For now, however, we will focus on one story and its effect on one little girl.

Imogen is six years old, and for six years, she has lived with the knowledge that she is 'different'. Imogen suffers from a condition known as albinism — a lack of the pigment melanin in her hair, her eyes and her skin.

'Albinos' exist in every race and culture, and are often made to suffer for their 'difference' through various measures of exclusion. This is due to the inherent human reflex of resisting the unusual, and is often not even a conscious response.

In the story, Imogen is used to people 'looking away'. She is isolated by her difference, and made to feel an outcast. Even by the age of six, she has developed a negative perspective towards herself and mistrusts her ability to fit in.

Addie's strength as a babysitter and a 'first best friend' lies not simply in her willingness to accept Imogen for the beautiful and delicate child she is. Rather, it is her skill as a storyteller and her gift of empathy, which allow her to transform, not the world, or the situation, but the little girl's perspective — her 'mindset'.

'*They changed the way I looked at myself...*' says Imogen, speaking of the stories. And, in the end, that is quite a good definition of mindset.

The way I look at myself...

The world is the world, and though we may 'chip away at the edges', we cannot usually change the way things are — any more than Imogen can change the colour of her eyes, her hair or her skin. What we *can* change, however, is the way we see ourselves *in relation to that world* — the way we *value* our unique natures. In other words, we can change our mindset.

Our children may not stand out, the way Imogen does — the sources of their insecurities may not be as obvious as pink, translucent skin and a shock of white hair — but all children doubt themselves, at times. They doubt their ability to succeed, to fit in — to be loved.

This section is about developing, in our children, a strong and resilient mindset — the ability to look at the world and see opportunity, and the confidence to grasp that opportunity with both hands.

Reflections

Of course 'the way I look at myself' is a little more complex than it might first appear. Many adults spend huge sums of money attending seminars and 'events', where they learn commercialised variations on these four simple truths:

1. **The world we see is a reflection of the way we see ourselves.**

2. **The way the world sees us is also a reflection of the way we see ourselves.**

3. **Our expectations are a reflection of the way we see the world.**

4. **Our outcomes are a reflection of our expectations.**

A very young child does not judge the world — or himself/herself. A very young child simply experiences.

Unfortunately, this does not last.

Over the past half-century, science and psychology have established, with great authority, that the way we, as adults, see ourselves and the world is strongly influenced by the views, the behaviours and the language of our parents and other 'significant figures' — by the mindsets we experienced, absorbed and internalised in our childhood, especially in our pre-school years.

Of course, this is a truth which far pre-dates modern psychology and scientific research.

> **An old Spanish proverb states:**
> **'More grows in the garden than the gardener sows.'**
> **An even-older Hebrew proverb puts it this way:**
> **'As is the gardener, such is the garden.'**

Being the parent of a young child carries a heavy responsibility, because our every word, our every action and our every response is being watched and listened to, and soaked up, sponge-like, by our children.

> **One of the truly exciting — and frightening — things about being a parent:**
> **We make a difference to our children's future mindset, whether we try to or not.**

Whether we try to or not...
So, why not try? Why not think about the mindset we want our children to possess when they go out to face the world — and set about modelling it for them to imitate?

Why not make the mindset they experience, absorb and internalise as a child the mindset of a champion? After all, the four simple truths listed earlier have four simple corollaries:

1. If they see themselves as capable and creative — as champions — then they will see the world as a place in which to express creativity and championship.
2. If they see themselves as capable and creative, then the world will tend to share that opinion of them.
3. If they see the world as a place in which to express creativity and championship, they will learn to anticipate success.
4. If they anticipate success, they will find numerous ways of achieving it.

'Winners' and 'Champions' — Are They the Same Thing?

If we are going to set the development of 'championship' as a goal for our children to aspire to, we must be very clear about what it means — and perhaps more importantly, what it doesn't mean — to be a champion.

A champion is not necessarily, or even primarily, a 'world-beater'. Coming first is the mark of a winner — but not necessarily of a champion. Champions win, certainly; in fact, they are famous for it, but they also lose. What sets them apart from mere winners is that they learn from both experiences.

Winning, in any sphere of life, is more-often-than-not a shortlived phase, but championship is a way of living your entire life.

> **Championship is a frame of mind — a way of approaching life that looks for the value not only in victories, but even in setbacks and 'failures'.**
>
> **It is the art of succeeding at whatever is important to you and enjoying the process — both the 'ups' and the 'downs'.**

Young children understand this concept instinctively. They love to succeed and even to win, but the important thing is to be playing — and learning.

Unfortunately, it is a fragile trait — a frame of mind which often does not survive the first few years of life.

It is adults, in general, who first become hooked on a child's 'results' — coming first; topping the test; winning the game/prize/trophy — while children (as they do in most things) follow their lead, narrowing their focus, until the need to compete and not the thrill of discovery, becomes the principal driver.

Then, the joy of doing devolves into a striving for the short-term goal — at which point, even if they win, they are, in a real sense, the loser.

> **As parents, we must remember that life is not a competition; it is a journey of discovery and wonder.**
>
> **We have the unique opportunity to help our children to capitalise on their innate strengths, to encourage their enthusiasm and their ability to learn from successes and setbacks.**
>
> **If we free ourselves from the tyranny of short-term goals and focus on the fundamentals, we are well on the way to empowering future champions by establishing, in them, the 'Champion Mindset'.**

A: Mindset

Laying the Foundations of Championship

> **Keep a green tree in your heart and perhaps the singing bird will come...**
> **— Ancient Chinese Saying**

Playground

At the centre of the small park, the playground sits, like a silent vortex, drawing into its orbit, from all the streets and tall apartment blocks which surround it, the children — and their trailing parents.

They come, these children — struggling against the restraining hand, the harness or the stroller belt —— eager to be free of the world beyond this circle of sand and magic. Staring up, as they approach, at the towering, silver slide; the three-swing gantry; and the spider's web of intersecting cables that form the domed climbing frame; they leave behind a world of rules and order, and give themselves to play.

Or do they?

Sitting on a bench, camouflaged behind the morning paper, you watch the ebb and flow of bodies in motion.

Suri, four and feisty, who shakes herself free of her mother's grip and strides towards the climbing frame, eyes focussed, chin set, and grasping the thick cables with purpose, as she begins her climb. No hesitation; no furtive looking down. No contemplation of failure — it is not an option.

'Take care,' her mother suggests, as she finds a seat beside you, but she is smiling. She takes out her book and thumbs it open, reading one-eyed, as her daughter climbs.

The words are a habit, only. And Suri knows it, turning to wave a tiny hand, mid-climb, already halfway to her goal.

While hovering, eyes down, at the edge of the sand-circle, Jayden makes a nest of his tiny fingers and falters.

'Join in,' his mother encourages, nervous hands on both his shoulders. 'I'm sure they're very nice. Come on, I'll push you on the swing.' But neither of them moves.

Sitting on her own, near the circle's edge, Dora lines up twigs, sticking them upright in the sand and counting as she goes, '3... 4.... 6...' The numbers have a meaning that she fails to understand, but it is important to say them.

'1... 2...,' she begins again. Mantra without meaning.

Practice makes perfect.

Watching from close by, her mother consults her watch. Five minutes more. Art class at two-thirty...

On the wooden platform, next to the cubby, Douglas spins the wheel of his imaginary galleon — a pirate, scanning the sand-sea for enemies, or victims, a parrot on his shoulder, his sails billowing with imagination.

While Arifah and Christina sit cross-legged on his deck, unaware of the impending battle, talking of dolls and fairy princesses.

And Simon sits by his father's side, watching from the safety of the bench — and listening to the one-sided cell-phone conversation.

'Three-twenty and no more. Tell him it's more than they're worth... Hey, sport, aren't you going to play? I've got better things to do than bring you here, if all you're going to do is sit there, like... Yeah, I know they are, but I'm not going any higher...'

High in the sky, the sun shines down, and the trees cast their umbrella shadows. You fold your paper and pause.

Confident, diffident, imaginative, literal, solitary and sociable, expansive and reserved — the playground draws them all...

The Elements of Mindset

Johann Wolfgang von Goethe, one of Germany's greatest thinkers, once wrote:

A man sees in the world what he carries in his heart.

Goethe was, of course, a genius of international repute, and his powers of observation were acute. Though he speaks, poetically, of the heart, modern science and psychology are essentially in agreement with him.

Our perception of any event or experience is coloured by factors which have little or nothing to do with what is happening around us, but everything to do with our pre-existing mindset — what Goethe calls 'the heart'.

Consider then, our playground full of pre-school children. Each child will have a different experience of this potential wonderland, based on where the child is in the playground, what each sees, hears, tastes, smells and feels — and what each misses.

How children interpret the evidence of their senses, however — including how they judge and respond to other children — will also be significantly affected by the influence of previous experiences. Even at this early age, the child's 'mindset' has been, and is being, influenced by:

- **Values and Beliefs**

  Is sharing important? Is it safe to trust others (outside the family)? Am I someone that other kids like? Is it okay to scream and make lots of noise like that girl on the swings? Is it okay to play with a boy/a girl/a Muslim/an Indian/a Caucasian/an Asian/a poor kid/a kid in a wheel-chair?

  Among the greatest influences on a child's values and beliefs — and, therefore, on his responses to the world around him — are the opinions, statements and behaviours of the 'significant adults' in his or her life. These influences, drawn from everything we say and do in front of our children, form the *accepted wisdom* about the world, which will colour every future experience.

  As parents, we are never 'off-duty', because our opinion always counts.

- **Internal Monologue**

  This is a term, coined to describe what I, as a normal human being, say to myself inside my mind — and sometimes out loud.

  This monologue is one way that most of us — including young children — make sense of a complex environment. The on-going commentary which we provide on the events of our lives — both important and mundane — is a vital process, but it can easily become hijacked by our emotions and our (sometimes misguided) beliefs.

  How children speak to their own self — both the content and the emotional tone — strongly influences their expectations and therefore their perceptions, of every experience.

  Including a trip to the park.

- **Dominant Senses**

  Children favour one or more of their senses, when taking in the world around them, and how they perceive the individual elements will be influenced by the few bits of sensory information (sounds, sights and

TALKING WITH THE SKY

smells etc.) which make it through to the conscious awareness — out of the millions of possible elements which exist in the playground environment.

- **Emotional, Physical and Psychological State**

  Think back to Maslow's Hierarchy of Needs in Chapter One. Children's reaction to the park, the playground, the other children — and even the weather — will inevitably be influenced by everything else that is happening in their life at the time, and it will show in their behaviour and in the level of learning and enjoyment they might derive from the experience.

- **Past Experiences**

  The template we carry around with us — a template against which we measure every new experience — is formed and constantly updated by all our experiences. It is this ability of humans to constantly learn from past experiences and to adjust behaviours accordingly that has made homo sapiens the dominant species on Earth.

  Positive, fun experiences at the park on previous visits will prepare a child for a fun afternoon, and s/he will, therefore, seek out — or recognise — fun experiences, both alone and with others.

  Of course, negative past experiences will pre-dispose a child to expect the worst — and the playground and its inhabitants will, more likely than not, appear to fulfil that expectation!

  As parents, the more pleasant, enjoyable experiences we create for our children in new environments, the more likely they are to create enjoyable experiences for themselves on future occasions in the same environment.

Memory and Emotion

As we grow, we record our experiences of the world as memories.

As soon as a newborn's recently-opened eyes begin to focus, and those tiny ears begin to make sense of the strange surrounding sounds, memories are created that lay the foundations of his/her mindset. Every experience and every input children receive from parents, family, siblings, total

114   Pre-school Parenting Secrets

strangers — and even the media — impacts on the way they will experience the world from that moment on.

Emotions are the most intense influence on our developing mindset. The experience of positive emotions such as love, security, happiness and confidence or negative emotions such as fear, insecurity and anger have a powerful impact on the development of our worldview.

> **Emotions serve to reinforce and anchor experiences, and to assign a subjective emotional meaning to events in our life.**

Emotions can change the meaning of an event and the way it is coded in our brain. Often emotions strengthen the template which will largely determine our future responses to similar events. Even the way we make meaning of language is determined by our own developing mindset.

Consider your child's early learning experiences.

The emotion experienced by your children during learning will affect whether they believe learning to be a positive or negative activity. This, in turn, will affect the mindset they apply to learning. For example, we may experience learning as a joyful and fulfilling activity, or as a distressing and frustrating one.

> **What beliefs, feelings, habits and/or emotional states associated with learning would you like your children to develop?**

There is much a parent can do to mould and change a child's mindset which can set them up for all their future experiences. Developing a positive, independent 'champion mindset' is the obvious place to start, if we are going to create positive and lasting change.

So, What Do We Learn from Observing a Group of Children at Play in a Public Park?

Much of the research into early-childhood development centres on the influence of parents and carers on the child's attitudes and learning habits. Researchers stress that much of what a child picks up is non-conscious — subtle body language; subliminal responses — emotions of which even the parent is unaware.

Now, let us revisit our afternoon in the park...

Suri, confident and adventurous, sets goals for herself and attacks them with enthusiasm, scaling her own miniature Everest one small step at a time. But, is her mother there behind her, ready to catch her if she falls?

Hardly.

Having assessed the risks, Suri's mother sits back, reading her book and allowing her child the freedom to achieve. However, in no sense is Suri's mother negligent.

While Suri has the freedom to explore her potential, her mother is there to act as a 'safety net', should she need one. She reads her book 'one-eyed', monitoring the situation at all times. She has confidence in her daughter's abilities, and Suri responds accordingly.

In Jayden, on the other hand, we glimpse a child who has absorbed his mother's hesitancy. He wavers on the edge of the sand-circle, reluctant to commit; desiring the experience, yet uncertain.

More than anything, Jayden's mother wants her child to become involved — to face the world with confidence — but her example is at odds with her words.

'Join in,' she says, as her hands on his shoulders hold him back.

'I'll push you on the swing,' she says — but she hesitates, unwilling to commit.

For Dora, the park is not so much an adventure as an extension of her carefully timetabled life. The book says 'free-play, especially outdoors', so her mother dutifully slots it in between the flash-card session and the artclass.

Dora sits alone at the boundary of the circle, not running, shouting, climbing, or exploring, her 'play' an extension of the habits she has been drilling — without too much understanding.

Does she mix? Does she imagine herself in a world beyond the here-and-now? Perhaps. Perhaps not. For Dora, there is little time to consider such things. The timetable is full and enrichment awaits...

As Douglas spins his wheel, he is transported. Is he reliving a scene from *Pirates of the Caribbean*, channelling Captain Jack Sparrow? Are his imaginings fuelled by a dozen re-readings of *Tough Boris* by Mem Fox and Kathryn Brown, or bath times inspired by Jarrett Krosoczka's *Bubble-Bath Pirates* or the sheer fun of Pamela Allen's *I Wish I had a Pirate Suit*?

Whatever the inspiration, Douglas' imagination is in full flight, and his everyday world is transformed.

So too for Arifah and Christina. While Douglas sees the deck of a pirate galleon, together they inhabit a fantasy world of magic and fairy princesses.

Is it real? Perhaps not. Are they learning anything important? Most certainly!

Like Douglas, Arifah and Christina have learned to move beyond the limitations of the here-and-now, to create ideas and possibilities — behaviours which are the hallmarks of creative thinkers. In play, they are rehearsing the skills which real-life will demand of them in the near future.

But what about Simon?

Trailing along in the wake of his father's busy life, he sits, without the confidence to explore or join in.

Does his father love him? Probably. After all, hasn't he taken time out of his busy life to bring him to the park?

And yet... The subtext in all we see explains the child's reluctance to enjoy the experience. He sits next to his pre-occupied father — desperate, perhaps, for the attention a busy lifestyle doesn't afford him. But even here, the phone — and business — take precedence. Sandwiched in between negotiations, he can't help but see himself as an imposition — a distraction that his father could do without.

Young children learn quickly to read the signs — of encouragement and of disapproval — that we send out, both consciously and unconsciously.

Which is why the playground means such different things to such different children...

To Do...

Consider your own mindset. What aspects of it would you like to pass on to your children? More specifically:

1. **What values and beliefs about learning would you like to pass on to your children, to create positive learning habits?**
   a. ***Example*** Min values new information and knowledge, and demonstrates this value through verbally expressing a curiosity in the world and local events. Her children see her reading newspapers, books and internet sites, especially about topics that catch her interest. She also enrols in short courses to improve her skills in both her hobbies and career. She talks about this with her children.

b. *Example* John has a belief that when he puts more time into a new skill he is learning, he gets better at it. His children watched him practise his basketball shot recently, as well as observing him revising his notes from his recent professional development day at work. He talks about this with his children. He hopes that when they go to school they'll also apply this belief to revision of work learned at school.

c. *Example* Tina sees organisation as a positive learning habit. She has taught her children to use a calendar to mark in important dates, in preparation for starting school and writing in when homework is due.

2. **What aspects of your mindset would you like your children to avoid — and how would you go about it?**
   Example Mary has strong natural ability and got through university with the mindset of leaving things until the last minute. This made her university experience very stressful, not to mention developing some bad habits. She would like her children to avoid this and has focussed on instilling in them a mindset of organisation and getting started on tasks early, by setting a good example and sharing her planning process with her children.

❦

B: Bouncing Back

How to Encourage Emotional Resilience in Your Child

Nature does have manure and she does have roots as well as blossoms, and you can't hate the manure and blame the roots for not being blossoms.

— Buckminster Fuller

Families today experience unhealthy levels of stress daily, and the incidence of childhood depression is increasing.

Stress and setbacks are an inevitable part of life, but children and adults can learn to cope effectively with life's obstacles and to combat depression.

Some people, no matter what setbacks befall them, always seem to bounce back, while others seem to be completely 'floored' by misfortune. Those who bounce back from adversity are described as 'emotionally resilient'.

Emotionally resilient people are more successful in school and careers, are healthier, happier, live longer, and are less likely to experience depression.

Reivich and Shatté, authors of the book *The Resilience Factor* (2002), wrote that resilient people are better able to deal with stress and adversity and overcome childhood disadvantage, and are more likely to explore new opportunities.

Resilience is clearly a desirable trait to possess.

Children with lower levels of emotional resilience, on the other hand, have been found to be at greater risk of poor educational achievement.[36]

The good news is that children, even at an early age, can be taught to challenge their previous thinking and learn cognitive skills that will develop emotional resilience.[37]

What Is Emotional Resilience?

Emotional resilience is the ability to cope, change and persevere when things go wrong. A resilient person is one who is able to recover quickly after a setback.[38]

A setback can be as simple as struggling to pile wooden blocks into a tower, or as profound as the death of a loved one. People — including young children — who are emotionally resilient, employ positive and optimistic thinking patterns to deal with life's setbacks.

Emotional resilience isn't necessarily something we're born with — but children can learn the cognitive skills that support resilience.[39]

Cognitive skills are activities such as thinking, reasoning, conceiving, imagining, fantasising and constructing a self-image. Every person has a unique cognitive style, which forms a part of their overall mindset. Cognitive psychologists work with patients to modify existing — and teach new — cognitive processes.

More than by genetics or intelligence, resilience is determined by thinking style — and as we will see, thinking style is something that we can influence, even in the very young.

So, it makes good sense to start to develop emotional resilience at an early age. When warm, caring adults foster realistic optimism and a positive worldview, the children around them develop lifelong emotional resilience.

Serena and Lonny have each received low marks in a test at school.

Serena is resilient and responds by saying, 'Well, I passed, which is good, but I'd like to do better next time. What can I do to ensure that I get the mark I want next time? Where did I do well and where do I need to learn more? Did I spend enough time studying?'

Lonny is less resilient and responds by saying, 'I knew I would do badly. I'm so dumb! I'm never going to do well in anything.'

Serena's response to the setback is motivating and leads to a positive action. Lonny's response is to just give up.

Lonny may well benefit from working with a cognitive therapist to help her develop more positive and resourceful thinking skills, thus increasing her resilience.

Of course (prevention always being better than cure), it would have been preferable if she could have developed a positive outlook from the outset — as your pre-schooler most certainly can.

Psychologist Martin E. P. Seligman, author of (among other ground breaking books) *Authentic Happiness (2002)* and *The Optimistic Child (1995)* describes the skills of emotional resilience extremely well.

Promoting Emotional Resilience Skills

Here are some key 'resilience skills' and some suggestions for how you, as a parent, can develop these skills in your children. We will discuss these in more detail later.

Skill 1: Impulse Control
What Is It?

Impulse control is best defined as:

- Learning how to 'wait'

- Avoiding being over-emotional or 'losing control'

- The ability to control impulses when we're emotional

Poor impulse control can lead to such problems as over-spending or violent behaviour in adolescence and adulthood.

How Do I Help My Child Achieve It?

- Calm your child down if s/he is about to lash out physically when upset.
- Encourage him/her to delay gratification by saying, '*Good things come to those who wait*' and (in a shop) '*You can't always have everything you want!*'
- In 'the heat of the moment', use strategies such as taking deep breaths, counting to 10… or just walking away.

Skill 2: Understanding Cause and Effect
What Is It?

Understanding the notion of cause and effect is a necessary skill, if we are to learn to master our impulses or plan future outcomes. It involves:

- Understanding where the responsibility lies in a given situation and, thus, whether it is within your control.
- The knowledge that volitional choices can and do change the outcome of any situation.

An understanding of cause and effect is essential not only in social and emotional circumstances. It underpins all logical thought in areas such as science, mathematics — and even literature.

How Do I Help My Child Achieve It?

Teach your children to take responsibility for their choices, and to understand that better choices create positive outcomes.

- If your child wants another child's toy, explain that simply grabbing it from another will probably just lead to a fight.
- Talk children through an 'I want it now' urge.

Every action, every choice has a consequence — it is a lesson that children learn through experience, so provide the experience and guide their growth.

Skill 3: Empathy
What Is It?

Empathy is the ability to understand the emotional experience of others by:

- Putting yourself in the other person's place.
- Being able to see yourself — and your actions — from another's point of view, and (using your understanding of cause and effect) assess the effect of your behaviour on someone other than yourself.

Young children need to learn to overcome their egocentric perspective. By helping them see other perspectives, you prepare them with an essential social skill.

How Do I Help My Child Achieve It?
- Give your child a wide emotional vocabulary.
- Teach him/her to read body language and facial expression.
- Teach him/her empathetic language such as '*I can see you are upset. Would you like a cuddle?*'

Our own resilience is strengthened if we learn to get on with others. Even at a very young age, human beings are gregarious creatures. We need acceptance almost as much as we need food. Empathy towards others triggers that acceptance, and this makes it an essential skill to build in our young children.

Skill 4: Perceptual Parallax — Seeing Other Points of View
What Is It?
Similar to empathy, perceptual parallax is the ability to see other perspectives — but in contexts other than the purely emotional. It is:
- The ability to stand outside ourselves and see the world from others' point of view, appreciating why they may think and feel differently from the way we do about a situation.

This is not a skill that comes easily to the very young, but we can give them practical, concrete experience of various perspectives — to begin the process of understanding the fact that perspective changes 'reality'.

How Do I Help My Child Achieve It?
- Play games with your child that raise his/her awareness of multiple viewpoints.
- Discuss differences of opinion or points of view with your child when the opportunity arises — such as '*Bananas are my favourite fruit, and apples are yours. It's okay to be different, isn't it?*'

Giving your child a wider perspective on the world helps in the development of creative thought and problem-solving. The ability to see possible solutions to challenging situations is an important resilience skill.

Skill 5: Self-Efficacy
What Is It?
Self-efficacy is defined as our belief in our own abilities underpinned by a healthy self-esteem.

- Resilience rests on the belief that I can achieve my goals and overcome the obstacles which life places in my path. Self-efficacy is a measure of that belief.

How Do I Help My Children Achieve It?
- Use 'descriptive praise' (see Chapter Four) to foster a healthy self-esteem in your children and reinforce the strategies which lead to success.
- Acknowledge your children's specific abilities and show them how to acquire the skills they need to succeed.
- Instil in your children that success in many endeavours is within their control — that 'Practice makes perfect'.

No life is without its challenges. Helping a child develop the mindset that turns 'upsets into setups' is an important way that you can build resilience in your child.

Skill 6: Self-Confidence
What Is It?
Children are more adventurous and stretch their 'comfort zone' more willingly if they have a healthy self-esteem and a strong support network.

- If Self-Efficacy is the belief that I have the ability to achieve success, then Self-Confidence is the belief that I am important enough to deserve it.

How Do I Help My Child Achieve It?
Rehearse situations which require self-confidence, and give your child practice in the process of behaving confidently. Try this one:

- Role-play approaching another child and saying, '*Can I play with you?*' and explore the various possible outcomes — including the other child saying '*No*'.
- Suggest possible responses to your child, such as '*Okay. Maybe I'll ask another time. But now I'll ask someone else, who might say 'Yes'*.

Self-confidence grows from knowing your own strengths. The more we get to practise our strengths and strengthen our weaknesses, the more confident we become.

Three Resilience Domains

Goldstein and Brooks, in their book *Raising Resilient Children*,[40] add another perspective to the development of resilience in children. They believe that there are three major domains that influence its development. They are:

i. Internal Resources

Internal Resources include:

- Developing an easy-going temperament
- Learning problem-solving and coping skills
- Having a higher level of self-esteem and a realistic sense of personal control such as those described in the Promoting Emotional Resilience Skills section earlier

ii. Family Culture

Family culture is a home environment where there is:
- Warmth
- Affection
- Emotional support
- Clear cut and reasonable structure and limits

This environment, and how it can be created, will be discussed in more detail later.

iii. Social Environment Outside the Home

The social environment outside the home consists of:
- Extended family members
- Friends
- Community groups
- Pre-school

All of which also provide support to the child.

A crucial element in these three domains is the presence of at least one adult in the child's life — whether it be a parent, grandparent, sibling, carer, coach or mentor — who provides unconditional love and support to this child.

This person is trusted by the child implicitly and provides support in times of both success and adversity. As Werner put it:

> **Most of all, self-esteem and self-efficacy were promoted through supportive relationships. The resilient youngsters in our study all had at least one person in their lives who accepted them unconditionally.**[41]

A Changing World Requires Resilience

Change is stressful.

As human beings, we have evolved to respond to the unknown partly through the release of stress hormones. In this regard, a little bit of stress is related to enhanced learning, due to the focussing effect of these hormones, and not only is it not a bad thing, it is actually beneficial.

Of course, like everything else in life, too much of a good thing isn't necessarily better. Too much stress produces anxiety, health problems, sleep disruption and an inability to store and recall information.

In a world that is changing as rapidly as the one in which we — and our young children — find ourselves, the stress levels can easily move beyond what is safe. Preparing our young children with the strategies to resist stress and stay focussed and positive — to become emotionally resilient — should be one of our highest priorities.

We can develop perspectives that promote realistic optimism and learn thinking skills that promote a positive view on the world. Resilient thinking and behaviour modelled by warm caring adults nurtures children's lifelong capacity for resilience.

To Do...

> **Opportunities to develop resilience skills in children happen throughout the day and are very effective when folded into normal daily events.**
>
> Consider the Emotional Resilience Skills discussed in this chapter:
>
> Skill 1: Impulse Control
> Skill 2: Understanding Cause and Effect
> Skill 3: Empathy
> Skill 4: Perceptual Parallax — Seeing Other Points of View
> Skill 5: Self-Efficacy
> Skill 6: Self-Confidence

Choose one or more of those skills to develop in your child this week. Let's imagine your focus for this week is on *Skill 5: Self-Efficacy*. For example, you notice that your child tends to become frustrated and say "I can't do it. You do it!" after one failed attempt when learning something new, such as tying shoe laces.

When this happens you could teach him or her that persistence and sustained effort lead to success. When children persist beyond initial failure, they eventually succeed and this success generates a more positive attitude about their ability to learn, which in turn formulates a belief that they are good learners (positive self-efficacy).

During learning, you could offer verbal encouragement and re-teach the skill such as "I know you're clever. All you need to do is to try again and again, until you get it right! Let me show you again. It always takes lots of practice when we learn something new".

If frustration reaches a peak, take some time away from the task and say "That's okay. Learning new things can be difficult. Let's have a rest and come back and learn some more when you are ready".

ᢀᢀ

C: Impulse Control and Life Success

How to Help Your Children Take Control of Their Impulses

A year from now you may wish you had started today.
— **Karen Lamb**

The ability to control impulses is an important life skill. It has the potential to impact the direction of a person's life in very significant ways.

A child with poor impulse control may struggle at school both socially and intellectually. Adults with mild impulse control problems may find it hard to resist over-spending on their credit card.

Prisons are full of people with a severe inability to control their impulses resulting in behaviours such as violent outbursts or theft.

Fortunately, impulse control is a skill that can be learned early in life.

It may seem that impulsivity often goes 'hand in hand' with pre-school children! Indeed, one of the greatest challenges for parents is helping their children learn to manage their emotions and impulses.

Luckily, there is much you can do as a parent to help your children learn impulse control.

A Famous Impulse-Control Experiment

In the 1960s, psychologist Walter Mischel, from Stanford University, started a 12-year experiment to show the advantages of impulse control for children.[42] In this experiment, a group of four-year-olds were each offered a lolly as a treat. If they were willing to wait for the adult (who was really the researcher) to run an errand, they would be allowed two lollies when he returned.

Some four-year-olds were able to wait what must surely have seemed an endless 15 to 20 minutes for the adult to return. To occupy themselves while waiting they covered their eyes so that they wouldn't have to stare at the lolly, or rested their heads in their arms, talked to themselves, and even tried to go to sleep.

These resourceful pre-schoolers got the two-lolly reward. But others, who were more impulsive, grabbed the one lolly, almost always within seconds of the adult's leaving the room for his 'errand'.

All of the four-year-olds in this experiment were tracked down 12 years later as they were graduating from high school.

The emotional and social difference between the two kinds of graduates — that is, the pre-schoolers who waited the 15 to 20 minutes, and those who ate the lolly within seconds — was dramatic.

Those who had demonstrated the ability to wait 15 to 20 minutes at four were now, as adolescents, more socially competent: personally effective, self-assertive, and better able to cope with the frustrations of life.

What Is Impulse Control?

All of us — adults and children — have impulses. An impulse is an urge to do something or say something; and we can either give in to that urge or we can learn to control it.

Take, for example, a child who wants another child's toy.

The child may give in to an impulse to take the toy, but s/he can learn to control that impulse.

Similarly, the child whose toy has just been taken may give in to an impulse to hit whoever took it, but s/he can learn to control that impulse. Having impulses is a natural part of being human; learning to control our impulses is an important part of living together.

Tonia Caselman (author of the invaluable 2005 book — *Stop and Think: Impulse Control for Children*) describes impulse control in this way:

Impulse control is knowing how to stop and think when we have an impulse. It is the power to freeze the impulse for long enough to think about whether it is a good idea or not to act upon it. Impulse control is like being the boss of your impulses [instead of their slave].'

How can Parents Help Children to Develop Impulse Control?

Below are five sets of activities that you can use to help your pre-school child develop impulse control. These activities were developed for school-aged children, but they can be modified to suit pre-schoolers.

Experiment with the games for a set period (say, six months) and track any changes in your children's ability to control their impulsive behaviour.

If, as well as a pre-schooler, you have children in Primary 2 to 7, you could also play the Impulse Control Game as a family. (The game can be ordered from this website: www.childtherapytoys.com.)

1. Develop a Vocabulary About Impulse Control

A child's first step towards developing impulse control is learning how to talk about it.

In particular, the child needs to be able to describe the differences between impulsive behaviour and controlled behaviour. You can help by explaining concepts such as thinking, waiting and being calm.

Talk to children about these concepts using simple language, as if you were talking about having a bath or eating breakfast. If you use simple positive phrases, eventually these will form part of an internal conversation that the child has with himself or herself. Examples of questions or statements you can introduce are:

- *'What is waiting?'*
- *'When do we have to wait?'*
- *'What can we do while we wait?'*
- *'Waiting is good to do, isn't it?'*
- *'It's my turn now, then it's your turn.'*

You can also help by explaining that you sometimes get frustrated waiting — just like they do — and suggesting ways to cope. For example:

- *'When I'm angry, I stand still, breathe gently and count to 10.'*
- *'When I'm angry, I walk away so that I can calm down. When I've calmed down, I think about things better and say things better.'*

2. Play Games Involving Impulse Control

Different types of games help children to develop different ways to control their impulses.

i. 'What if...'? Games

These games help to develop impulse control because they require the children to imagine a particular situation and to ask themselves how they would act in it if it were real.

They explore the concept of 'Cause and Effect', where choices can lead to positive or negative outcomes. Imagining the outcomes of various choices in advance — for instance, choosing to snatch another child's toy — gives your child a 'virtual' experience without the bruises!

Asking children 'What if… ?' can help them to change the way they see things and change the way they react to situations.

'What if…?' games help children learn how to control their impulses because when children imagine themselves coping with a difficult situation, they are well on the way to coping with that sort of situation in real life.

Here are some examples of how to start a *'What if…'* game:

- *'What if your friend took your favourite toy away from you?'*
- *'What if you had to wait a long time for your turn in a game?'*

ii. Board and Card Games

Board and card games help to develop impulse control because they require us to take turns, that is, to control our impulse to win by preventing anyone else from playing!

Suitable games for playing with pre-school children include *Snap, Memory* and *Snakes (Chutes) and Ladders*; you may also have others at home.

iii. Role play

Role plays help to develop impulse control because they require the child to imagine what it feels like to be someone else who might be affected by the same impulses. (In this way, role play games are a bit like 'What if …' games.)

To create a role play game, choose a scenario that involves impulse control, then act it out with your children, with each person playing a different role — good and bad. At the end, discuss what you each learnt from playing each role, about controlling impulses.

iv. Mazes
A maze is a fantastic way to help children develop impulse control because it requires them to look ahead and think about consequences before they act.

Children can rely on impulse to solve the maze, but they are far more likely to be successful if they control their impulses and ask themselves at each turn in a maze, 'If I make this choice, will it take me to the end of the maze?'

3. Use Stories to Explore Impulse Control
Stories help children to control impulses because they often involve both the reader and the characters waiting for things to happen.

For example, in the fairytale Little Red Riding Hood, the Wolf has to wait a long time for Little Red Riding Hood to arrive at her Grandma's cottage, and we, as readers, have to wait to see the outcome of his being there.

As you read a story to your children, ask them to predict what they think might happen — and why. This is a fun exercise in applying cause and effect, because the children are already hooked into the story. It also helps children to maintain concentration and engagement, because they are waiting to see if their prediction comes true.

Also, while you are reading, point to any examples of a character showing impulse control, or a lack of it, and ask your children how they would act in those circumstances.

4. Use a Calendar or a Watch to Show Time Passing
To control our impulses, we must understand that time passes and that eventually it will be the right time to do what we want to do impulsively.

However, young children can find it hard to understand an abstract idea like time passes while we wait. One way to help them is to use something that shows time passing — such as a calendar or a watch.

You can use a calendar to show your child how time is passing as s/he waits for a special event, such as visiting a friend or relative, going on a holiday, or celebrating a festival.

By putting a star on each day that passes, children can see the special event getting closer and closer as they wait.

A watch — especially an analogue one (with hands and numbers) — can be used for more short-term situations, like this one:

'We have to wait half an hour after we eat, before we can go swimming. That's when the big hand reaches the 6. You tell me when it's time, in case I don't notice.'

This strategy also prepares your pre-schooler for the important skill of telling the time. When we understand the purpose of an activity — when it has meaning to us — we learn it more quickly and more effectively.

5. Praise Examples of Impulse Control

Make sure that you praise your children when they show impulse control, because this tells them that you are pleased with how they are behaving.

Often, we give children feedback when they have done something bad, as a means of correcting behaviour. Feedback is attention. Sometimes this sends a message to children that attention comes when they are badly behaved.

Make it your mission for one week to mainly give your child feedback when they are behaving well. We call this *'catching them doing something good'*.

As an example, when you see them take turns, wait, share, calm down, walk away from a fight or resist taking something that does not belong to them, show them that you have noticed this and that you are pleased with it. You can do this by making comments such as:

- *'I noticed that when you got angry with your brother, you just walked away instead of yelling at him. That was really good!'*
- *'I saw you stop yourself from running in the house. Well done!'*
- *'Well done for waiting!'*
- *'You are learning to take turns — that's great!'*

Growing Out of Impulsive Behaviour

Although impulsivity seems to be a trait of pre-schoolers, as parents we can do much to help our children 'grow out of impulsivity'. Experiment with the suggestions above and notice the development in your child.

To Do...

1. You may like to try the 'lolly' experiment with your child to see how much Impulse Control they already possess.

2. What behaviours did you observe in your child this week that showed Impulse Control? Did you praise him/her at the time?

3. What activities might you do with your child to develop his/her Impulse Control?

◦✿◦

D: Points of View

Strategies to Help Your Child See through the Eyes of Others...

> **What is a weed? A weed is a plant whose virtues have not yet been discovered.'**
> — **Ralph Waldo Emerson**

In order to make and maintain relationships, solve problems and resolve conflict successfully, humans need to develop the ability to see the world from others' perspectives.

Unfortunately, young children find it hard to recognise that not everyone sees things as they do.

Their limited experience means that they can only see things from their own point of view and not from anyone else's.

They sit where they can see the television — even though no one else can; and they ask someone questions while they're engaged in an important phone conversation. They assume that other people see and hear what they see and hear.

According to Jean Piaget,[43] this happens because pre-school children are 'egocentric'. Egocentricity in young children is not about selfishness, but an inability to perceive things from another's point of view.

> **It is important to remember that egocentricity is not an abnormality; rather it reflects a normal cognitive processing limitation that diminishes with age.**

Most children simply grow out of it. You may be surprised to hear, however, that we do not actually lose our egocentric tendency by adulthood; we just get better at acknowledging and fixing it.[44]

Adults are able to take a 'mind leap', which demands significant cognitive effort, to then go on and view the situation from a perspective that is not their personal viewpoint.

We can do this because cognitive processes become faster and more automatic with practice and experience, so, logically, the older you are, the better your skills.

Indeed, in experiments, the older children were already less likely to commit egocentric errors than the younger children.

The good news is that, as parents, the more we can help our children practise seeing the world from alternate points of view, the more we will increase their ability to correct the egocentric impulse.

Mastering multiple viewpoints develops empathy and emotional intelligence — two attributes which are widely believed to be greater indicators of life success than intellectual intelligence.[45]

Seeing the World through Your Children's Eyes

Our earlier discussion about 'Mindset' tells us that no two people — especially parents and children — have the same perspective on any situation.

We also know that it is the adult who has the refined ability to imagine and anticipate other people's viewpoints — which is particularly important to keep in mind when children find themselves in trouble.

We must be aware of our responsibility, as the mature party, to find solutions, control the emotion and engineer a positive result. A good approach to apply is Stephen R Covey's 5th Habit:

First seek to understand, and then to be understood.

Remember that, very often, a child's reason for committing some 'unacceptable' behaviour may be perfectly logical and 'acceptable' — or even necessary — from their inexperienced or limited perspective. So before over-reacting, be sure that you are both talking about the *same* incident.

Remind yourself that your child's point of view and yours might be radically different — for very good reasons. Approach the incident in a calm, supportive manner, rather than an accusatory one.

This way you stand a good chance of understanding the motivation behind the action — which might never come out if the situation spirals into confrontation.

> **Always start with the request,
> 'Tell me what happened.'**

First, Second and Third Positions

As you teach your child to master alternative points of view, you may find the work of Grinder and DeLozier[46] helpful.

They have developed a clear way of describing the three different perspectives from which a person can view the world — which they call First, Second and Third positions.

Many people are very adept at one position (their own), but not so good at taking another. The best understanding comes from experiencing all three. As a parent, having this information is extremely valuable in your quest to teach your children to master alternative points of view.

» The First Position: 'Self'

This can be defined as *your* reality, your own perspective on any situation. Being aware of your own stance — and possessing the self-awareness to understand at least some of the reasons behind it — is essential.

Unfortunately, too many people confuse their own perspective with 'the truth'. This implies that no other perspective — or opinion — is valid.

Working with the three positions teaches a child from an early age that other people's views can often be very different — but it is a lesson which emerges very slowly. Don't expect miracles. Your role in the pre-school years is merely to lay the concrete foundations for this very abstract understanding.

» The Second Position: 'Other'

Mastery of this position requires empathy and rapport. It demands the ability to use your imagination to understand the world from another person's perspective. It requires that you 'think as they think'. Assuming the Second Position enables us to appreciate other people's feelings.

There are two types of Second Position:

1. **Emotional Second Position:** understands the other person's emotions. You don't want to hurt them because you can imagine their pain.

2. **Intellectual Second Position:** understands how another person thinks, the kind of ideas they have and the sort of opinions and expectations they hold.

While such abstract sophistication is largely beyond the reach of your pre-schooler, by practising 'point-of-view' exercises (see *Playing with Viewpoints below*) at a concrete level – 'What can bear see?' or 'What would it look like to a mouse?', you prepare the ground for a later growth in awareness and the ability to assume the Second Position.

» The Third Position: 'Observer'

The Third Position demands the ability to step outside your view and the other person's view to a detached 'neutral' perspective.

From Third Position, you can see the relationship between the two viewpoints. Third position is important when you wish to check the fairness of your outcomes. You have to forget for a moment that it is your outcome and that you want it, and look at the situation in a more detached way.

Again, when we consider the notion of Third Position in relation to pre-school children, we do not expect such a sophisticated ability to compromise. We can prepare our children for a future mindset which is open to compromise.

All we need to do is to approach each childhood confrontation or argument as an opportunity to encourage them to see both perspectives and discuss ways in which they may be resolved so that everyone is happy.

Storytime is often a great opportunity to look at different perspectives — especially in picture books. Discuss why the Big Bad Wolf

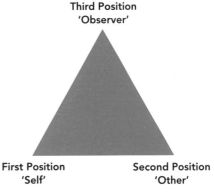

Third Position
'Observer'

First Position   Second Position
'Self'   'Other'

First, Second and Third Positions

might want to eat Red Riding Hood, or why the children in *The Cat in the Hat* might have a different reaction to the Cat's idea of fun from their law-abiding gold-fish's.

Your children can more easily see the different perspectives if they are not emotionally committed to one. This is what makes stories so valuable in this context.

The Third Position is the path towards compromise, and it is never too early to set a child's feet firmly on that track.

Playing with Viewpoints

Through practice and experience, young children can overcome egocentricity and see people, problems and conflicts from multiple points of view. It won't happen overnight, but it will happen!

Here are five activities you can do with your children to assist them in this endeavour.

1. Explore Your Home from Different Viewpoints

Ask your child, 'How many ways can you see this room?' Or, better still, place soft toys — like Rabbit, Bear, Ducky and Pup in different positions, and ask questions like *'What does rabbit see?'* or *'Look at the photo of Daddy — can bear see it from where he is sitting?'*

Help them, by sitting or lying with them, so that they have the same perspective as the animal — and can see what the toy 'sees'. Get them to stand on the table (if safe!), sit under the table, crouch in the corner or lie on the floor. Ask them, *'What do you see?'* and *'What does the room look like now?'* Encourage them to ask you similar questions.

2. Make a 3D Object

Draw a different picture on each side of your object. Place the object at the centre of the table, sit opposite your child, and ask them, *'What picture do you see?'* and *'Do you see the same picture as I do?'*

Remember to count to three mentally to give your children a chance to answer! Your children's short-term memory is still developing, so they may need to practise remembering what is on each side of the object.

3. Celebrate Differences of Opinion about Little Things

When small differences arise, celebrate them by saying, for example, *'I like tea, but you like fruit juice. It's good to be different sometimes, isn't it?'*

4. Role Play First, Second and Third Positions

When children bring you a problem — *'My friends said I couldn't play with them today'* — role play the situation. Do it several times to ensure that each of you plays both parts — so that you each take the First and Second Positions. Then take the Third Position together and discuss the situation.

5. Make Puppets and Watch Your Child's Puppet Show

In a good Puppet Show, the puppeteers know their characters and all the audience can see the action! So, children need to adopt their characters' viewpoints; and they need to position their puppets where the audience will see them — which requires them to learn that the audience will see the puppets from a perspective different from theirs.

It is empowering, as a parent, to know that you can do something practical to help your children socialise, solve problems and resolve conflict. It's also good to know how easy it is to develop their empathy and emotional intelligence.

Take a gentle approach and understand that cognitive development takes years — but be confident that the more fun practice you give a child, the more the behaviour will become ingrained.

To Do...

> Enjoy the suggested 'point-of-view-building' exercises presented above.

❧

E: Knowing When to 'Step Back'

How to Let Your Children Flourish

> **All gardeners need to know when to accept something wonderful and unexpected, taking no credit except for letting it be.**
>
> **— Allen Lacy**

GRACIE

The beam is a foot or so above the rubber playground floor of the local pre-school. With her arms outstretched in a four-year-old's wobbly imitation of an Olympic gymnast, Gracie is balancing on the beam, a look of intense concentration fixed on her tiny face.

But four-year-olds have a scant understanding of physics. Or of gravity. After a few moments of teetering, Gracie falls from the beam, bumping her head and grazing her elbow. A reflex cry of fright escapes, before she realises that it doesn't hurt all that much, after all.

Mrs Lee, the duty teacher, shakes her head, smiles and moves across to the scene of the accident. Leaning down, she holds out her hand, to help the child up.

"That's okay, sweetie. Up you get. Let's take a look at you... No bruises, up you get on the beam again. You can do it. You'll have that gold medal in no time."

Following her adored teacher's lead, Gracie steps back onto the beam and gingerly takes some steps.

"That's it!" Ever the cheerleader, Mrs Lee claps her hands a few times, as her eyes stray to watch the boys throwing a ball against the wall. 'A few more steps and you'll have your confidence again. You–"

Her words of encouragement are interrupted by Gracie's panicked mother, June, who witnessed the incident from the carpark and has come running over.

"Gracie? Are you hurt, baby? Let me see. Oh dear..."

Her newfound confidence deserting her, Gracie immediately freezes on the beam and starts to cry.

"It's too dangerous for you. Off the beam please — we don't want any more falls." Still talking to the child, June turns to glare at the teacher. "People in positions of responsibility really should take more care."

June means well. After all, isn't it a parent's role to protect her child — to ensure the child doesn't get hurt?

Of course it is. But there is a fine line between protecting and over-protecting — a line which June has just crossed.

Most parents would agree that they want to see their children grow into well adjusted and self-sufficient adults, but many find it hard to 'let go'. Barbara Burrill of Positive Parenting believes the reason for this is because it leaves parents with a sense of loss:

> **'There's no more pleasing love,' she writes, 'than that of a pre-schooler who relies so much on the security of the home for his own feelings of safety. As they grow up, bit-by-bit they relinquish that and bit-by-bit parents feel a sense of loss. The whole process of growing up is kids pushing to be let go and parents struggling to determine when is it right to let them go.'**

The Media and Parental Anxiety

As parents we are constantly confronted with images of children in danger in the media, in reports of childhood accidents, abuse and neglect. These images are distressing and anxiety-inducing. It is little wonder that parents can develop an over-protective attitude toward their children in their quest to keep them safe from all these dangers.

The 'Sometimes Risky' Physical Nature of Early Childhood Learning

Pre-school children interact with the world in a very physical way, exploring their environment and practising physical mastery.

This physical mastery has a strong connection to their self esteem.[47] All parents who have witnessed their baby taking those first tottering steps will know how filled with self-pride and excitement a child is at the accomplishment.

Pre-school children need the opportunity to physically master their world, because this sets up their beliefs about their ability to master other obstacles and challenges in their lives.

However, this does not mean that children are the best judges of the risk involved in any activity or that parents should not be cautious. The trick is to be able to balance, as a parent, the need to allow children to try and fail — with a few bumps and bruises along the way — and prevent them from experiencing serious physical harm.

Every parent knows that 'heart in your throat' fear of watching your pre-schooler about to tumble over!

How Do I *Know* If I Am Being an Over-protective Parent?

High levels of fear and anxiety in parents can cause over-protective behaviour toward their children. There are a number of specific behaviours over-protective parents tend to display.

If you're having difficulty in letting your child become more independent, you may want to ask yourself if these questions apply to you.[48]

Do you:

- see every physical activity as potentially dangerous?
- feel the need to constantly watch your child in order to feel safe?
- hover over your child, continually issuing instructions?
- forbid any activity that has even a remote possibility of causing an accident?

A good gauge for judging if you're being over-protective or balanced is to ask yourself the questions parenting expert Mary Gordon formulated to identify over-protective behaviour:

- What are the other kids of a similar age doing?
- How are they coping with it?
- Is my child behaving like the other children or not?
- If my child isn't doing the things the others are doing, how can I help prepare him to be able to?

Gordon states:

We don't do our children a favour by holding them back if they are ready. We do them a favour to make them ready.

Can Being Over-Protective Harm Children?

Parents who are fearful for their children's safety can reduce their children's confidence and self-esteem. Over-protecting children only makes them more dependent and less adventurous and makes them far less likely to do things by themselves.

Over-protective parents reinforce in their children the belief that they can't deal with challenges and that every new activity and experience is dangerous.

However, children are less likely to fall or injure themselves when left alone to play than when parents constantly oversee their activities and intervene. The time to warn a child about the dangers inherent in an activity is before they engage in it — not while it is taking place!

Parental interference during an activity only serves to distract and disturb — increasing the chance that a lapse of concentration will result in an accident.

Remember too that the language we use to draw our child's attention to a potential danger is very important. There is strong anecdotal evidence that warnings like *'You might slip'* or *'Be careful you don't fall'* are likely to become a kind of self-fulfilling prophecy.

Young children are very concrete thinkers. The instruction *'Don't fall'* or *'Don't slip'* doesn't carry any information on how to avoid those outcomes — all it does is focus the child's limited attention on the notion of falling or slipping — thus increasing the likelihood of that outcome occurring.

> **A more effective approach is to phrase the warning in terms of the behaviour you wish to occur, rather than the one you wish to avoid.**

'Walk in the centre of the path, because the edges are muddy' is an instruction that carries all the necessary information, and it is easy for a child to follow – as is 'Hold onto the railing as you go down the steps'.

Concrete instructions — desirable results.

When children do something on their own for the first time, such as balancing on a beam or riding a bicycle, it represents a great source of healthy personal pride. Being an over-protective parent denies children these crucial experiences and may hinder their growth into independent, confident adults.[49]

In our playground example, June's anxiety and fear caused an over-protective reaction to the situation. While other parents were more than happy to allow their children to experiment in the playground, because it was a safe environment and the teacher was very skilled and experienced, June was indignant that she had been forced to save her child from what she perceived to be an obvious danger.

Unfortunately, denying Grace the opportunity to get back on the beam robs her of the opportunity to succeed. June also risks instilling in her daughter a sense of fear and failure (a failure which becomes anchored in the playground equipment which she sees almost every day) — a constant reminder of the negative lesson.

How Can Parents Avoid Being Over-Protective?

If you suspect that you are over-protective, ask other parents for their opinion. You need not adopt their opinions, but they can at least help you to make an informed decision about what is safe for your child.

You should also ask your children for their opinion. Tell them that you believe that they can look after themselves, but nonetheless you are concerned about their safety. Discuss the dangers of particular activities and advise your children how to cope with them. Make your judgements based on your assessment of your children's competence and judgement.

Despite adopting these measures, there will still be occasions where parents may still deny their children permission to participate in an activity. This is a parent's prerogative — and duty — and has the weight of experience and superior judgement behind it.

What is safe and acceptable for one child may not be so for another. Parents are the best judges of what activities are acceptable for their children in terms of safety. However, the children will realise that while they may be denied this particular pleasure, there will be other activities that will be permissible.

Over-Protective or an Advocate?

Protecting children from the consequences of their actions may be essential when there is real physical or psychological danger involved, but most of the time, our over-protective urges are triggered as much by a fear of 'failure' as by a fear of physical danger. By never allowing children to fail, we deny them the lessons which will enable them to cope with failure.

Professor Allan Snyder of Sydney University's Centre for the Mind goes further. In his book, *What Makes a Champion!* he writes:

> **Surprisingly, what emerged from our research is the possible necessity of overcoming adversity as a preparation for being a champion, even adversity created by oneself, say in setting goals beyond reach.**[50]

Pre-schoolers will, if left to their own devices, constantly set goals which are 'beyond reach'. How else, for example, would a child ever learn to walk — or talk? Overcoming adversity — solving problems, learning from mistakes — this is how human beings learn and grow. Over-protecting our children denies them this growth opportunity. As parents, some of the most difficult tasks of all are not the things we *do*, but the things we *don't do*.

Over-Protective Parental Behaviours to Avoid:
- **Denying a child the right to choose** (Most choices are harmless — get out of the way and let him/her choose!)
- **Being the sole authority on the selection of friends** (The ability to gauge people's personalities and make decisions based on that ability is one of the key measures of Emotional Intelligence. It is a skill that is only learned by trial and error — with the emphasis on the latter!)
- **Fighting all of a child's battles for him/her** (Choose the battles you think your children can fight for themselves and step back! You'll be pleasantly surprised at how well they do — and how quickly they overcome a setback.)
- **Censoring all risks from a child's life** (The ability to assess and balance risk and opportunity is an essential skill in a changing world, and the role of parents is to strengthen the children's belief in their problem-solving ability. A child who masters the notion of cause and effect early is a child who is prepared for the world beyond childhood!)

What a child needs is not a 'protector' or bodyguard, but an advocate.

An Advocate:
- **Empowers a child to make *his/her own* informed choices**, monitoring the consequences, but intervening only if those consequences threaten to bring on real personal danger.
- **Grants a child the right to take on the world** and plants the belief that success is a real and achievable — though not inevitable — outcome.
- **Identifies the internal 'road-blocks' to success** which can lead to a child becoming '"stuck" in a failure cycle'[51] (be it emotional, social, academic, and so forth) and provides workable alternatives to choose from.

What is safe and acceptable will always be a bone of contention between parents and children, but the important thing is for parents to realise that sometimes they just need to stand back and let go.

Letting go is hard to do. But helping our children find independence in an age-appropriate manner will, in the long run, help them grow into confident, independent adults.

To Do...

1. How would you rate yourself on a scale of protectiveness towards your children? (Please circle.)

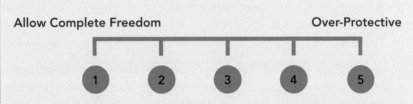

Allow Complete Freedom   **Over-Protective**

1   2   3   4   5

2. What do you fear most concerning your child's safety?

3. How do you manage your fears so that you enable your children the freedom to explore and learn?

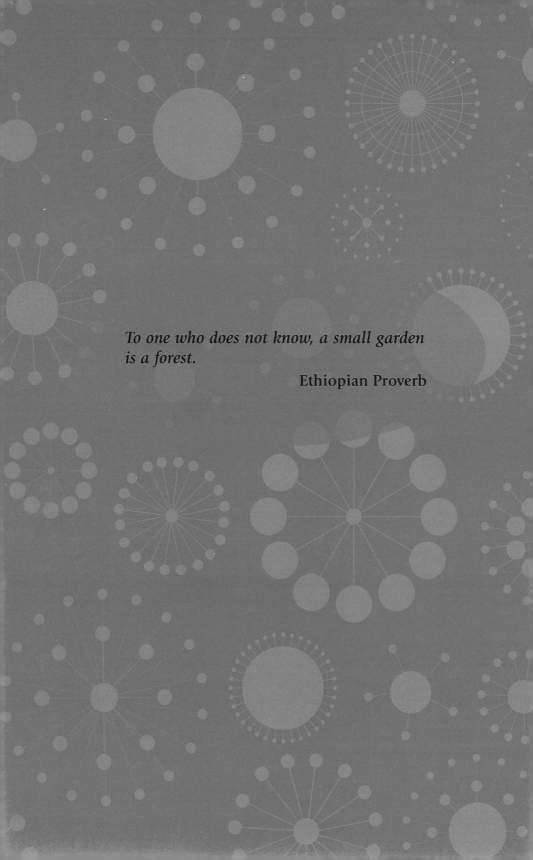

*To one who does not know, a small garden
is a forest.*

Ethiopian Proverb

THE SOCIAL NEEDS

Fostering Effective Communication and Social Skills

'Come on, Oliver. You can do it!'

The words of encouragement sound strident, but it could just be the embarrassment. You can feel the eyes of the whole room boring into your back. Are they watching Ollie or are they laughing silently at your increasingly futile efforts to coax out of him a performance he clearly has no intention of delivering?

Turning to the captive audience, you finally capitulate.

'Stage fright,' you offer, by way of excuse. 'With all the preparations going on, he didn't get his afternoon nap. He normally loves doing it. He giggles, and...'

'Shut up,' you tell yourself. You're just making it worse... But the void needs filling. Family are okay, but some of these people are work colleagues and you are beginning to imagine the whispers around the water-cooler.

'Never work with kids or animals...,' Uncle George to the rescue. 'They'll up-stage you every time!'

In 40 years on the stage, he's probably experienced far worse — if his war stories are to be believed. The shared laughter breaks the tension and you seize the opportunity to beat a face-saving retreat.

'I think it's bedtime for this little up-stager,' you announce, sweeping him off his feet and carrying him over the heads of the guests towards the stairs.

Across the room, Celia offers her 'I-told-you-so' smile, as she plays hostess with the crackers and dip.

This time, she did. Tell you. But you just didn't want to listen.

'He does it every time,' you argued, when she issued her prophetic warning. 'He's a natural performer.'

'For you. When you're alone. It's different with a group of strangers.'

You should have listened, of course. Celia comes from a big family. She understands the dynamics.

Yet another disadvantage of being an only child...

Up in the bedroom, you strip off his 'good clothes' and pour him into his pjs, tickling him, as you do, in a ritual that developed months ago, without you really noticing. He giggles and the embarrassment you have been feeling evaporates.

'Into bed,' you begin, but he doesn't move. He is staring at you expectantly.

'Do you still want me to do it, Daddy?'

'Of course, I do, kid,' you say, sitting down on the end of the bed. 'Knock yourself out.'

So he does. And he's brilliant, of course...

Cultivating Communication

> I know that you believe you understand what you think I said, but I'm not sure you realise that what you heard is not what I meant.
>
> — **Robert McCloskey**

'What is the best way to communicate with children?'

The 20-something father asked the question, with one eye fixed on his four-year-old, a boy with more energy than a kennel full of puppies — and about as much idea of what to do with it. The boy was clambering over a padded red sofa in the foyer of our Singapore office, with a Transformer toy in one hand and a melting chocolate biscuit in the other, headed for the activity room, where one of our trainers was reading a story to a group of rapt pre-schoolers.

The young father's question was a deceptively simple one, and it would have been easy, of course, to answer with a few glib adverbs: 'honestly'; 'calmly'; 'patiently' — 'often'. But ultimately, it is also one of the most important questions that a parent can ask, and as such, it deserves far more.

We are our children's role models for effective communication. What we say, and, importantly, how we communicate, is of crucial importance for their language development and for the development of their worldview, and it is not a responsibility to be undertaken lightly.

What is the best way to communicate with children?

Perhaps, in the end, it is to remember that communication is a two-way street. That we communicate *with* them, not *to* them.

If we are to create a home environment that supplies our children with the raw materials from which they can construct a Champion Mindset — if we are to help them to develop the communication skill set which most experts agree will be their most valuable asset in the world of the 21st Century — then we must provide the example.

And it is not as difficult as you might think.

Read on to find out how you can do it...

⊙⊹⊙

A: The Four Golden Rules for Inspired and Inspiring Communication

Learning and Teaching Champion Communication Skills

> **Be sincere; be brief; be seated.**
> **— Franklin D. Roosevelt**

A major part of our role as parents is to inspire and guide our children, especially at times when they are under pressure. To do this successfully, parents must keep open the channels of communication between themselves and their children.

Strong communication within a family:

- Enhances Attachment and Bonding between parents and their children
- Develops a child's sense of belonging and their self-esteem (remember Maslow's *Hierarchy of Needs* from *Volume One*?)
- Increases a child's Emotional Intelligence and Resilience

In *The Art of Communicating with Your Child*,[52] we created four 'golden rules' of communication between parents and children. We will now look at how these 'golden rules' apply to your pre-school child.

Golden Rule Number One
Be Aware of the Young Person's 'Processing Limitations'

Pre-school children have not yet developed the strategies to cope with complexity and stress as well as adults. The pre-frontal cortex of their brain is still developing, and they are far more likely to respond with their 'unthinking' emotions than with their logical faculties, when challenges arise.

» It's All About 'Networking'

This is because all our responses to the world are cued by previous experiences. Each new experience creates more neural connections within the developing brain — or reinforces and strengthens existing ones.

These 'networks' of connections give us the capacity to process and understand more and more complexity as we grow in experience.

Young children, however, have far fewer experiences to draw upon, so their ability to process complex or numerous ideas is limited. For this reason, the responses which are 'hard-wired' into the brain at birth have far more influence than they will in later years.

These 'hard-wired' responses are predominantly emotional (fear, anger, frustration, satisfaction [of drives], happiness etc.) and physical (pain, pleasure, tension, relaxation etc.). It is through experiences which trigger these emotions that children gradually develop:

a) *An understanding of how things work*

b) *The ability to interact with the world beyond themselves in a way which increases the number of positive experiences and reduces the number of negative one*

This is the essence of all human learning, and it is particularly important in the area of social behaviour.

» Controlling the Situation

As the adult, you must be the one to control the situation and avoid creating unnecessary frustration. Inspiration is about empowering the young person to achieve and you can do this only if you are communicating effectively — and without emotional misunderstanding.

To enable and encourage your children to face their challenges successfully, you need to communicate with them in ways that are unemotional, yet sensitive to their emotions and — perhaps more importantly — their capacities.

Asking two questions in quick succession, such as '*What are you doing with that? Why did you get it out of my cupboard?*' will more than likely cause a young child to 'short circuit' — both cognitively and emotionally.

If you are lucky, young charges may be able to answer one of the questions, but more likely they will 'freeze' or stutter as they start to formulate an answer to the first question, only to have the thought process interrupted by the second.

As adults, we have the 'parallel-processing circuitry' to be able to handle both questions simultaneously and then order our responses. It is a necessary skill for a complex and fast-moving world, which we have developed through years of practice and experience.

Your young child has no such luxury. S/he has barely mastered the meaning of the basic English vocabulary, let alone the nuances of tone and emotion that can subtly affect that meaning.

Think of it like this:

> Someone has just told you his/her phone number, and the pen has been moved from its normal place beside the phone, so you are trying desperately to hold it in your short-term memory, by repeating it over and over. Eight digits — nothing more — but you are at your maximum capacity.
>
> Suddenly, your eight-year-old, who is dutifully doing his homework in front of the TV, asks, 'Mum, what's 8 times 12?'
>
> The question is not a difficult one, but your brain, occupied as it is with the first task, is unable to process both bits of information simultaneously. In such a situation, its response will probably be to process the more familiar information — 8 times 12 — as this is a familiar routine, and the brain is drawn to the familiar. Unfortunately, this will

mean that the phone number you were trying so valiantly to hold on to disappears forever into the ether of unstored factoids.

How do you feel? Frustrated? Angry at your innocent son? At yourself and your own inadequacies? At whoever moved the pen?

Whatever your response, it is likely to be an emotional one.

» The 'Stock Response'

Young children face this dilemma constantly — especially when adults forget their processing limitations and talk to them at an adult level of complexity. For young children, 'doubling up' on questions often comes across as aggressive and threatening, even if that is not the intention, and the stress that this produces increases the child's feeling of 'overload'.

If this situation occurs regularly, they may develop a stock response, such as 'I don't know,' or even 'I didn't.'

Let's return to the original double-barrelled question: 'What are you doing with that? Why did you get it out of my cupboard?' Clearly, neither of these stock responses is an adequate answer.

Unless s/he is sleep-walking, your child clearly has an idea of what s/he is doing with the object and a reason why s/he got it out of the cupboard in the first place, but the questions were not delivered in a manner which is likely to elicit that reason.

Is your child telling you a lie? Semantically, yes. They do know the reason and most certainly did take it out. But at a more basic, cognitive level, the response is not so much a lie, as a circuit-breaker — a valve to release the pressure of cognitive overload that the questions have created.

Your interrogative technique has triggered an automatic 'stock' response, which a child is no more able to control than a cough or a sneeze.

As adults, we do a similar thing, when we are confronted with a question which tests our capacity. We don't 'lie' necessarily — we have more experience at being 'caught out'.

What we do is to apply a delaying strategy. We say, 'Pardon?' or 'I didn't quite catch that,' or 'Could you repeat that?'

We are, in a sense, lying, as we did, in fact, hear what was said, but getting the other person to repeat it gives us the extra time we need to process the answer. Some people even use the technique of repeating the question, as if they are confirming it.

Regardless of our technique, it is an automatic response.

Now that you are aware of it, listen for how different people 'buy time' with automatic responses in everyday conversation.

Look at things from your children's point of view, and you will understand their response, but if you react to a 'lie' with anger or disappointment, then the conversation becomes about the lie, not the original incident, and you have made your own day — and your children's — unnecessarily complicated.

Of course, children's processing limitation is not restricted to emotional issues. If you ask pre-schoolers, 'What is the first letter of the alphabet? What does it look like?', the same confusion and neuronal misfiring may well occur, and you are likely to get the same 'I don't know' response — even if they have been drilling the alphabet at home for weeks.

Party Trick

This is the same mechanism which causes the universal social embarrassment which has frustrated parents since the beginning of time.

Think about Oliver and his father.

Oliver was encouraged to perform his 'party trick' — the same one he had performed dozens of times when they were alone — but this time it was 'in public'. And what happened? He got an attack of 'stage fright'.

The problem wasn't that he couldn't 'do the trick' — or even that he didn't want to.

The problem was the same one you encounter with the double-barrelled question. Cognitive overload.

When they were at home alone, he could put all his limited concentration capacity into performing the trick for his adored father — which he was more than willing to do, because he liked the positive, encouraging response he always received. In the social situation, however, there was far more going on — far more to occupy the same 'head space' — leaving insufficient working memory to accomplish the 'trick'.

Luckily, most of the people in the room — if they were parents themselves — had been through similar embarrassments and understood, at least instinctively, that 'kids will always make a fool out of you'.

Remember, communication is as much about perception as it is the meaning of the actual words. If, from the child's perspective, your 'doubling-up' of questions is perceived as aggressive, then, in terms of the meaning conveyed, it is aggressive — no matter what your intent.

And the phenomenon is not limited to pre-schoolers. Research at the University of Minnesota shows that even by adolescence young people are still poor at 'multi-tasking'.

When asking questions, you will elicit information better one point at a time. A rule of thumb is to ask one question, and then count to three in your mind — '*One* 1000, *two* 1000, *three* 1000' — to give your pre-schooler time to answer.

» Showing Respect to Your Child

We are all aware of times when children neglect to show us respect, but are we as diligent in our observation of our own behaviour — especially during conversations with them?

Just as doubling-up on questions over-stretches children's limited capacities, interrupting their answer has the same effect. If we anticipate — or respond to — our children's answer or statement before they are finished, we run the very real risk of derailing their train of thought and confusing/frustrating them.

You have asked the question, or requested a response. Show your child the respect of listening to that response, before commenting. Be aware of the miracle that is taking place, as your child musters together the necessary memories, thought processes and language to answer your query, and understand how fragile that combination of elements is.

Your interruption may be calculated to assist, to expand understanding — even to support him/her — but its effect is to confused, disorient and frustrate. The child is in 'talk' mode. All of his/her faculties are focussed on the act of synthesising information into a spoken response. There is simply no more RAM left in his/her under-resourced computer for the 'parrallel-processing' required to listen to you as well.

» To Sum Up
When talking with your children:
- Ask just one question at a time
- Allow the young to finish speaking, instead of attempting to anticipate their answers
- Avoid the temptation to interrupt their answers, even if the words suggest a response

Golden Rule Number Two
Give Your Full Attention to All the Possibilities in a Communication Situation — No Matter What the Distractions

Confidence is the key to success. By far the best way for a parent to build confidence in young children is to show respect and to acknowledge that they are important and that what they have to say is important.

We cannot hope to guide or inspire, if our children think we do not care — or that their concerns are not important enough to warrant our total attention.

Whether we are communicating face-to-face, or just wish our children to know how we feel about them, focussing on all manner of communication modes is the key to effective inspiration.

» Paying Attention

If you are reading or watching TV, stop and make it obvious that you are stopping willingly to talk about something 'more important'.

Communication is primarily an emotional activity. By stopping what you are doing and giving your child your full attention, you are giving the right emotional signal to open up strong communication channels.

If it is impossible to talk at the moment your children approach you, it is important that they understand that it is no reflection on their importance, but simply a result of circumstances. Following up on the conversation as soon as possible afterwards reassures children, and shows that you respect them and their issues.

» The Power of Touch

Young children are very kinaesthetic. A touch or a hug can communicate as much positive emotion as any words.

Social signals can be confusing — especially for the young — but the meaning of a touch is generally unambiguous.

A hand laid softly on the arm or the shoulder; the back of the fingers touching or running softly down the cheek; holding the child's gaze while taking his/her head gently in both hands and drawing him/her towards you until your foreheads meet; a protective hug in times of high emotion — these are almost universally effective gestures of love and support, even (especially) in families which traditionally have not employed them.

One common symptom of dysfunctionality within a family is the inability of family members to display warmth and affection through tactile displays.

» Smiling

Most people underestimate the power of a smile. A smile opens up the channels of communication — even with total strangers — because it communicates at a non-conscious level.

From birth, our children are actually 'hard-wired' to respond to a smile with positive emotion. It banishes fear or insecurity and says, '*I am here for you. Nothing you have to say can change the way I feel about you.*'

So remember, whatever you want to say to your child, begin with a smile…

» Find 'Private Time' for Important Moments

The best time for communication between you and your child is when no one else is around. It means the child only has to focus on one person, without splitting his or her attention.

Only involve other parties if there is some specific reason why they need to be involved. Young children feel less 'pressured' one-on-one.

» To Sum Up

When you wish to really communicate with your child, or when they really want to communicate with you:

- Pay attention to the conversation and to your child as an important individual
- Be free with hugs and other tactile signs of affection
- Teach yourself to smile
- Maintain a sense of privacy between you and your child

Golden Rule Number Three
Provide Support While Encouraging Independence

> **If you hit a wrong note, it's the next note that determines if it's good or bad.**
> **— Miles Davis (Jazz Legend)**

'Empowerment' does not mean doing everything for your children — it means giving your children the guidance and confidence to back their own judgement. It is an important part of preparing a young person for the demands of the world. The more your children come to rely on you, the less able they will be to rely on themselves.

» Guidance — Not Dependence

When presented with a challenge facing our child, it is by far the easiest approach to use our experience to create a solution, which can then be given directly to the young person. Problem solved.

If we know an answer, the quickest and least demanding response is to provide it, so that things can move efficiently onward. If we see our children making a mistake, it is natural to 'set them straight' immediately — even forcefully — to avoid the inconvenience, embarrassment or extra work that the mistake might produce.

But is it the best approach?

Remember the role of the parent is that of 'guide' — not oracle, dictator or 'fairy godmother'. If the young never have to solve problems or deal with adversity or consequences, how can they learn how to react to such events, when you are no longer there to solve everything for them?

During times of disappointment or crisis, let your children know that you still love and support them, no matter the result, and 'failures' will not assume such a world-swallowing importance.

The research of Professor Allan Snyder indicates that being able to cope with and embrace the learnings provided by setbacks and adversity is one of the key markers of championship and your support during the process is great for a child's morale.

In **What Makes a Champion!** Professor Snyder writes:

Champions are often familiar with adversity. They have had to 'fight' to get where they are... They learn how to convert... 'upsets into set-ups'... Struggling in the early learning process possibly acclimatises us to difficulties, and may advantage us in dealing with adversity [later]. What has emerged from our research is the possible necessity of overcoming adversity as a preparation for being a champion.

Show that you will help if they need you to, but don't offer or try to solve every problem for them immediately.

» Gradually Introducing Responsibility

By assuming accountability one small step at a time, young people learn to develop responsible attitudes. They feel more useful and valued, and invariably respond positively. To learn responsibility, they need to practice being responsible.

Your example is important, of course, but you wouldn't expect anyone — even an adult — to learn to drive just by watching you. Observation gives them the basic principles, but they need to sit behind the wheel and 'get a feel' for the gears, the brakes and the steering, if they are ever going to become accomplished drivers.

Responsibility, like driving, is a 'hands-on' skill.

» To Sum Up
When assessing your child's performance or achievement when dealing with challenges:

- Show that you will help if they need you to, but don't offer or try to 'solve' every problem for them immediately
- Gradually introduce responsibility to your children.

Golden Rule Number Four
Develop Strategies for Controlling the Negative Emotion in Any Situation

When emotions (yours or the child's) create a barrier to resolving a situation, it is important to have strategies in place, to 'defuse' the moment.

i) **Especially in times of crisis, or when they might feel that they are 'in trouble', don't 'stand over' your child.**

Posture, as we will see later, is a key indicator of relative power. Standing over your child may well win reluctant obedience, but our aim is to guide and share, rather than dictate and dominate. Instead, physically try to get down to your child's level (crouch, sit on a low stool or on the floor), then talk. For an excellent example of this approach, watch a really good kindergarten teacher in operation.

ii) **If you are very upset or angry about a behaviour or an incident, allow some 'time out' to calm yourself and regain control before 'dealing' with the incident.**

Emotional responses are never as effective as considered ones. Though you might feel the need to address the incident immediately, it is far better to deal with it effectively and with a positive resolution, than to take action that is fuelled by unmanaged emotion.

> **As a guide, it takes about 20 minutes for a heightened emotional state to subside, as long as there is an absence of further aggravation.**

Send the child away on his/her own, to think about what has occurred, and then find a way to disperse the anger before discussing the incident. This will allow for better communication, and it will also allow time for the child to reflect on his/her behaviour too.

Many of our young children's actions are taken 'on the spur of the moment', but immediate confrontation — before they have had the opportunity to make a considered analysis of the full implications of those actions — forces them into a position of 'defending' their behaviour.

iii) Avoiding the 'Why?' question

Don't ask 'Why?' as your first question. 'Why?' is usually interpreted as an accusation demanding an excuse and puts the child on the defensive.

Begin by simply asking the child what happened. The 'why' will follow naturally, but without 'forcing' the justification — which may be 'cloudy' at best.

Alternatively, you can use phrases like 'Tell me all you can', or 'How did you feel?' Questions which draw out the truth without accusation reduce the level of 'threat' the child is feeling and lead to a resolution far more efficiently than threats and badgering.

> **The child's primary need is to feel loved and accepted, and if telling the truth is what achieves that result, then the truth becomes the preferred option.**

Consider this four-point checklist for defusing an explosive situation:
1. If necessary, resolve the 'public' situation first. As long as others are involved, it is more challenging to get to the truth, as the emotional 'interference' is too distracting.

2. Give the child time to consider the situation without confrontation.

3. Take steps to get to the 'real story' — the intent or influence behind the action.

4. Resolve the situation in consultation with the child. Unilateral decisions are rarely satisfactory — for either party — in the long run.

iv) Dealing with a Lie

If your child is lying, or likely to tell a lie, and you have prior knowledge of the situation, inform the child that you have information on the incident and ask him/her to think for a few minutes about what occurred before telling you what really happened. Don't try to use information to 'trap' a child in a lie. Accept the fact that human beings lie — especially if they are inexperienced children with an incomplete notion of cause and effect. You are interested in getting to the truth and finding ways to resolve the issue — not in scoring cheap points in an imaginary competition. The key to preventing lying in children is to be consistent in the strategies you employ to deal with incidents — and with lies.

v) Avoiding the Ill-Considered Question

Remember, questions have the power to dictate the direction of the conversation. Be careful that the question you ask is leading in the direction you wish to go. Young children are literal by nature, so keep your questions simple and to the point. Above all, avoid the use of sarcasm and irony, as they rely on saying one thing, but meaning the opposite — which is conceptually beyond your pre-schooler. It may make you feel better to be clever and witty, but in the long run, it hampers communication with the young — though they will pick up the underlying contempt. After all, their non-conscious emotional radar is far superior to their abstract reasoning capacity.

» To Sum Up
When dealing with a negatively charged emotional situation:

- Develop strategies to avoid 'standing over' your child
- Use a 'time out' to regain emotional control

- Find alternatives to the 'why' question
- Develop strategies for preventing — or dealing with — lying
- Consider the power — and danger — of the ill-considered question

Communication isn't rocket science — it's much more complicated. But it doesn't have to be an emotional minefield, especially when you are communicating with someone small — someone you love more than anyone else in the world.

The four 'Golden Rules' aren't so much about what you say to your child, as how you go about saying it. Remember, the words you use are less than 10% of what you communicate in any conversation. These rules help you to think about the other 90+%.

To Do...

1. Experiment with the information about questions. As an experiment, deliberately ask your children two or more questions in a row and observe their response.

2. Then, practice the 'one question at a time rule' with your children. Note the differences.

3. Reflect upon how often you display physical affection to your children. How does the information about 'touch' fit with you culturally and personally?

B: The Simple Art of Saying What You Mean

Language Strategies for Parents

The more elaborate our means of communication, the less we communicate.

— Joseph Priestley

As a parent, you might, once or twice, have found yourself making a comment — something like this:

'My child never seems to do what I ask! He always seems to do the very thing I ask him not to do!'

Well, you may be surprised to find that your child may have actually been doing exactly what you asked all along! Read on to uncover a simple language strategy that can help all parents to communicate more effectively with their children.

The Pre-School Years Are a Time When Language Blossoms!

During pre-school years, children experience rapid language acquisition. As they learn about the world, they experiment with language by 'trial and error'.

Every parent knows how delightful it is to be around pre-schoolers who are experimenting with their newfound and fast-improving language skills. Learning language is a skill that occurs so naturally, and yet it is neurologically very complex.

Consider that all humans first learn language by associating images of objects and living things with sounds. The brain creates an internal image of a thing and connects it with the sound.

Once learned, the information is stored in our brain, ready to be called up as needed. For example, once children learn and store what a tree is, you could ask them, 'What is a tree?' and they will access their created internal image of a tree and begin describing that particular image.

What is really interesting is that if you said to children 'Do NOT think of a tree!' they will still bring up an image of a tree in their mind. Once the object, thing or idea has been spoken, the mind automatically responds by accessing that image.

Try this experiment — I'm going to ask you NOT to think of a juicy mango. Did you just recall an image of a mango in your mind, even though I asked you not to?

Of course you did!

The Non-conscious and Conscious Minds — When 'No' Means 'Yes'

The human mind has long been discussed in terms of having two main 'divisions' — the 'conscious' and the 'non-conscious' (or subconscious, or unconscious — the terms are quite imprecise).

Alternatively, we could think of the conscious mind as the General and the non-conscious mind as the Soldiers who follow the orders of the General — most of the time.

> **Using the analogy of a computer, the non-conscious mind is like all the software programmes and files stored on the hard drive. The conscious mind is like the desktop — including the document or file you are actively working on at the moment.**

The non-conscious mind is the storehouse of all the information that we have learned throughout our lives — and of all the automatic behaviours and reflexes which have been 'hard-wired' into us by our genes, through evolution.

Our conscious mind selects information from the non-conscious storage depending on what is needed. For example, all the language we acquire is stored in the non-conscious mind. So, when a child learns that an object with brown bark and green leaves is called a tree, the internal image and sound for 'tree' are stored in the non-conscious mind.

Only when we're actively thinking and talking about a tree — or if we happen to be surrounded by trees — will the information we know about trees appear as if by magic into the conscious mind. It is important that our mind is organised into non-conscious and conscious, because it would be impossible to consciously think of all the things we've ever learned in our lives all at the same time — we'd go crazy!

> **We simply don't have the capacity (the RAM) to think of everything we know. It would be the equivalent of opening up every programme, every document and every file on your computer simultaneously — the CPU gets instantly overwhelmed, and the system freezes.**

Apart from the 'day-to-day housekeeping tasks' of constantly monitoring the body's condition and states, and adjusting and fine-tuning every aspect of our physical function, the non-conscious mind has many other roles.

For example, it is designed to follow instructions in a direct, literal, non-judgemental and almost 'robotic' way. It does not make decisions because its job is to store and present information as requested. The non-conscious mind is also the storehouse of the imagination and emotions. There are so many functions within the non-conscious mind that it is no wonder scientists believe it accounts for more than 90% (some say more than 99%) of our brain's functions.

Of all the things the non-conscious mind can do, there is one thing it does not do very well, especially when a human being is very young.

The non-conscious mind does not understand the words 'not', 'no' and 'don't'. So when we instruct it not to think of a tree, it still brings up an image of a tree.

Likewise, when we ask it not to run, it will think of running and send impulses to our legs to run. Luckily, as we get older, our lifetime of experience trains the conscious mind to become good at interpretation — at quickly 'flipping' the instruction to read:

'If I shouldn't run, then I should walk…'.

When children are young, however, they are inexperienced, so they have not yet developed this ability.

So, How Do We Say What We Mean?

Understanding how young children's non-conscious mind works in relation to language will greatly assist the way we communicate with them.

When we grasp that young children's non-conscious mind has not yet developed the ability to 'flip' an instruction containing a 'not', 'no' or 'don't', we can quite easily change the way we give an instruction or ask a question. We can assess whether we have asked what we want them to do or what we don't want them to do. Consider the following example of how to change the common instructions we give children to ensure we state what we want, and not what we don't want.

When I say…	*'Don't run in the house.'*
My child hears…	*'Run in the house.'*
So now I say…	*'Walk in the house.'*

There is an art to 'saying what we mean' to young children, and you will be happy to know that it is easily learned. By stating what we want, we are using more positive language which will ultimately make communicating with our children far easier.

To Do...

Write down three frequent requests you make of your child, which include 'negative' phrases. Re-write them using positive language, saying what you want, and ensuring you take out words such as 'don't', 'not'and 'no'.

To begin with — until it becomes 'second-nature' — try using this three-step approach. It helps us to become consciously aware of the effect of our language on younger ears.

a. **When I say:** _____

_____

My child hears: _____

_____

So now I say: _____

_____

b. **When I say:** _____

_____

My child hears: _____

_____

So now I say: _____

_____

c. **When I say:** _____

_____

My child hears: _____

_____

So now I say: _____

_____

C: Self-Fulfilling Prophecies

How Your Child Lives Up (and Down) to Your Expectations

> **A tree does not move unless there is wind.**
> **— Afghan Proverb**

Pre-school children, on average, spend between 20 and 45 percent of their waking hours at pre-school, yet teachers are thought to be enormous influences on children's development and future academic success.

So, how do children spend the remaining percentage of their waking hours outside of pre-school — including time spent with their parents?

We still look to teachers to determine our children's future directions, but it may surprise you to learn that, according to a 2001 Michigan Department of Education report, parental expectations are among the most consistent predictors of children's future academic success, and, significantly, the earlier that parents become involved with their children's education, the greater their effect.

Expectations Create Results

For decades now, educational research has shown consistently that teachers' attitudes, beliefs and behaviours can influence a student's academic success enormously. That tradition of research started over 40 years ago, with the publication by Robert Rosenthal and Lenore Jacobson of *Pygmalion in the Classroom*. It was a very influential book that generated hundreds of follow-up studies. Rosenthal's and Jacobson's original study is summarised below. While its focus is teachers' expectations, its lessons apply to parents, too.

Rosenthal and Jacobson conducted their research in a public primary school. At the beginning of the school year, they gave the students an IQ (intelligence quotient) test. They told the teachers that the test not only determined students' intelligence but also identified 'academic bloomers', that is, students who would make rapid, above-average intellectual progress in the coming year, whether or not they were currently 'good' students.

After the test was administered, Rosenthal and Jacobson then gave the teachers a list of the 'academic bloomers' the test had identified. In fact, the test did not identify 'academic bloomers' — the researchers had just selected the names randomly from the class list. In short, any differences between these children and the rest of the class existed only in the teachers' minds.

At the end of the school year, Rosenthal and Jacobson gave the students another IQ test, and the results were — to say the least — significant.

The students whom the researchers had labelled as 'academic bloomers' increased their score by an average of more than 12 points, while the remaining students increased their score by an average of eight points.

The difference in scores was even larger in the early grades: almost half of the 'academic bloomers' in First and Second Grades increased their score by 20 points or more!

Teachers' subjective assessments (e.g. reading ability) of students showed similar differences, and the teachers reported that the 'academic bloomers' were better behaved, were more intellectually curious, had greater chances for future success, and were friendlier than the remaining students.

The following graph shows the startling difference in IQ gains between children labelled as 'academic bloomers' and others in First Grade (i.e. the youngest students).

On the basis of their results, Rosenthal and Jacobson concluded that the teachers had subtly and — perhaps unconsciously — encouraged the students to perform as they expected them to. They spent more time with the 'bloomers', created warmer relationships with them and were more

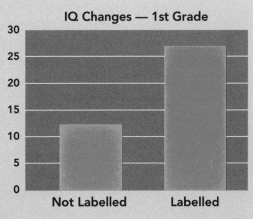

enthusiastic about teaching them. As a result, the 'bloomers' felt more intelligent and more capable of achieving academic success, and this led to their improvement in performance.

In other words, the teachers had created a self-fulfilling prophecy: they believed that the 'bloomers' had more potential than the other students, which led them to instil that belief in the 'bloomers', with the result that their scores improved significantly (especially the younger students). In the same way, the teachers believed that the 'non-bloomers' had less potential to succeed; they instilled that belief in the 'non-bloomers', with the result that their scores improved significantly less than those of the 'bloomers'.

Kate

In a related incident, the story is told of a young teacher — we'll call her Kate — who was struggling with a particularly boisterous and uncooperative class.

One day, while she was in the principal's office, the principal was called out for a moment, and she noticed, on his desk, the personal information file for her 'problem class'. Unable to resist, she sneaked a peek, keeping one eye on the door as she did so.

In the column which listed the kids' secret IQ scores, a shock awaited her. All the kids in the class — without exception — had scores above 130!

In a flash, she realised that the problem was not with the students, but with her own methods.

Why didn't they tell me? she thought. *I'm obviously not challenging them enough. They're acting out because they're bored...*

Armed with this new revelation, she made it her goal to learn all she could about gifted education — how to challenge and motivate children with high IQs.

Before long, things had begun to turn around. The students were more motivated, they were handing in work, doing their own research, and sharing jokes with her. They had become the dream class that, given their talents, they should always have been.

At the end of the year, the principal took Kate aside and congratulated her on the amazing improvement shown by her charges.

At that, Kate admitted what had happened.

'I know I shouldn't have looked,' she said, 'and I know that IQ scores are secret, but when I saw them, I realised that I had to challenge them. And it worked,' she finished proudly.

The principal looked puzzled.

'But...' he began, 'we don't keep the IQ scores in that file.'

When they consulted the folder again, the mystery was resolved, and Kate went white.

In her haste that day, she had glanced at the numbers, without checking the headings.

What she had mistakenly assumed were IQ scores were the children's locker numbers!

Young Children Behave As We Expect Them to Behave

In Rosenthal and Jacobson's research, the children responded to their teachers' expectations of them, but we can generalise and say that children — like adults — will respond to the expectations of any significant people in their lives.

Consciously or not, we give children clues (some as subtle as frowning slightly or subtly raising an eyebrow) as to what we believe and expect of them. Children, being the sensory radar machines they are, pick up on these clues about our expectations and act accordingly, because they really do want to do what we expect of them.

Young children like to listen to what adults say about them, and, because young children are literal thinkers, they often take those comments as absolute truth. Parents' comments enter a young child's non-conscious mind as suggestions about how to behave.

We saw in the previous section how important it is to be aware of the child's literal mind — a mind that absorbs information without the filter of experience and takes everything at 'face value'.

In a young child's non-conscious mind, comments like *'She's a poor listener'*, or *'He's bad at language'* become tacit commands and can create their own 'self-fulfilling prophecy'.

They say, in effect, *'I'm a bad listener, so I can't/shouldn't listen.'*

In the same way, when parents make positive comments about their children, these too can have very powerful effects.

Decades of research show that when parents are involved positively in their children's education, the result is increased motivation and self-esteem, leading to higher grades.

If you show your children that you believe in their abilities, that you expect them to do well and that you will help them if they need it, you can influence their academic success significantly.

Children respond far better to support and encouragement than they do to demands or pressure.

The following three activities have been shown to enhance children's success:

1. **Helping children with activities and homework in a calm, positive and supportive way**

2. **Demonstrating the learning habits you would like your children to have (e.g. starting a task early, rather than leaving it to the last minute, or choosing to read a book, rather than watching TV)**

3. **Reading to (and with) children and discussing what you have read**

Of course, none of these insights is exactly new. Already in this book, we have quoted the wisdom of Johann Wolfgang von Goethe, the great German writer and thinker. At the turn of the 19th Century, he wrote:

> **Treat people as if they were what they ought to be, and you help them to become what they are capable of being.**

We owe it to our children to see in them all that they have the potential of becoming.

To Do...

Reflect upon the beliefs and expectations you have of your young children. What are your hopes for their future, and what do you plan to do to help them?

a. I believe that my child is capable of....

_____

_____

b. I expect my child to achieve.....

_____

_____

c. I plan to help my child by...

_____

_____

❦

D: The Art of Praising and Criticising with Honesty

Simple Language Strategies for Parents

> **Applaud us when we run, console us when we fall, cheer us when we recover.**
> **— Edmund Burke**

Our self-esteem grows as a result of our interactions with others, from the day we are born until the day we die.

As we have learned from Attachment Theory and Maslow's Hierarchy of Needs, one of the key sources of self–esteem and self-image for children is the home. The way children feel about themselves is largely dependent upon the feedback they receive from significant adults in their lives. This means that parents' role as 'self-image facilitator' for their children is a crucial one.

One key way parents can increase the self-esteem of their children is through praise. But this cannot be achieved simply by pouring out a constant stream of unfounded praise.

Children know when praise is deserved — and when it isn't. False or excessive praise is patronising and potentially damaging to children. At best, it is a meaningless and slightly embarrassing ordeal for the child — especially if encountered in public. At worst, if used constantly, it creates an expectation of undeserved reward — which feeds on itself, creating an escalating demand cycle.

This is the universal 'spoiled child' syndrome, familiar to too many parents.

These parents, who have made the mistake of relying on unfounded praise and reward strategies to 'build up' their child's self-esteem, often find themselves looking desperately for ways to counter the ever-more-demanding behaviour of their children.

To impose an artificial self-image on a child by providing false praise or unearned rewards is not an uncommon mistake. We want our children to feel good, and we want to protect them from hurt or failure — but as we have already seen, a little failure can be a good thing — it teaches strength and resilience.

Self-image is constantly evolving and fragile, and we must be aware of how our actions and words affect it. True praise — praise which has its roots in a child's honest efforts — is a powerful reinforcer. Token praise reinforces too, but what it reinforces is not necessarily what we intended.

Of course, as parents, we cannot 'balance' over-praise by offering harsh criticism to keep our children 'humble' either. Both praise and criticism need to be delivered in an honest and respectful way so that the child may develop a healthy self-awareness, self-esteem and self-image.

There are two simple ways a parent can learn to positively praise and criticise children — by using 'descriptive praise' and 'constructive criticism'.

The Use of 'Descriptive Praise'

If a child has gone to some extra effort to do a job well, parents should also put in a little more effort in recognising the particulars of the good job the child has done. It requires that the parent notice the details of the work completed and be able to comment on some of those details.

Descriptive praise means that you are *paying attention* and, for most young children, that is a reward in itself.

> *'Alan, this castle is sensational. I love the way you've balanced these thicker blocks on top of the thin ones — I don't know if I could do that without them tipping over. And I love the way you've used the colours up the walls. It's very cool. By the way, did you pick up the leaves like I asked? It saves me a lot of time when you help me like that.'*

is much better than

> *'That's great, Alan. Now, did you pick up the leaves, or am I going to have to do it, as usual?'*

Parental approval is a significant motivator in people of all ages, and descriptive praise implies genuine approval.

1. It is not done 'just for the sake of it'.

2. It acknowledges effort, recognises ingenuity or creative problem-solving.

3. It has the effect of positively reinforcing the extra thought or effort that has been put into accomplishing a (sometimes) everyday task.

The feeling of achievement created by descriptive praise will encourage a willingness to earn more in the future. This is because the emotional reward that is tied at a subconscious level to the praise, creates an anchor to the behaviour that has just been praised.

Constructive Criticism — Using 'I' Statements, Rather Than 'You' Statements

Criticism can hurt, because even at a young age, we don't like to 'fail'. If handled in a positive and constructive way, however, criticism can actually help build self-esteem and relationships.

Constructive criticism is a positive way to offer criticism because it encourages growth and development. Giving constructive criticism to a child involves using an 'I' rather than a 'you' statement, and giving reasons for your criticism or 'demands'.

There is a subtle difference between using an 'I' statement ('*I really feel that…*') and a 'you' statement ('*You have caused 'X' to happen, because…*').

An 'I' statement focusses the young person on the effect a behaviour/ situation has had on you, whereas a 'you' statement comes across as a criticism of the person, rather than the action.

'I would really love it if you could help Mummy pick up the toys. It saves me a whole lot of time vacuuming if everything is away and I've got a clear floor to work with.'

works a whole lot better than

'This room is a pigsty. How could you leave it like this? If you don't tidy this mess up in the next ten minutes, I'll…'

Threats create negativity and conflict — especially as the child probably doesn't see the 'mess' as a problem in the first place. If you make it a problem, then it is *your* problem, and though a child may comply with your demands it will be with some confusion or resentment and reluctance.

If children have a *positive* reason to recognise the required change in behaviour, that is, it will make you happier, then they will be more motivated to improve their behaviour.

To Do...

1. Reflect upon the type of praise and criticism you commonly use as a parent.

2. Practise 'Descriptive Praise' at home using the following script to assist you with the method.

   '____(Name)____, this _____ is _____. I love the way _____ — I really feel I _____. Did you mean for _____? By the way, how was your _____ today? Anything you want to talk about?'

3. Practise 'Constructive Criticism' by using the following script structure to assist you.

   'I would really like it if you could _____this weekend. It helps me _____
   _____.'

E: Positive Discipline

'Spare the Rod' — and Promote Self-Discipline in Your Children

> **Enough shovels of earth — a mountain.**
> **Enough pails of water — a river.**
> **— Chinese Proverb**

In the very young, a lack of 'discipline' is not only natural — it is often disarmingly endearing.

From pulling all the books off the bookshelf, to extending their painting from the easel to the walls, to squeezing the cat until it squeals and runs away to hide under the stairs — these early behaviours are often so amusing to parents that they make great dinner party stories. But there is a point when parents become concerned about the behaviours and ask, 'How do we stop him/her from doing that?'

Aristotle once wrote:

What it lies in our power to do, it lies in our power not to do.

and three centuries later, Horace advised:

Rule your mind, or it will rule you.

Another 2000 years on, their words still ring true — for mature adults.

But, of course, babies are not born with any awareness of 'good' or 'bad' behaviour; they just explore their environment — touching, tasting, smelling and hearing — in a free and random way. They are easily re-directed if they run into danger, touch an item of value or are about to cause harm. Parents can simply pick them up and move them away without much protest.

At about 18 months of age, however, this strategy begins to lose its effectiveness, because toddlers have an emerging 'sense of self', independence and will-power. They want to continue doing what they are doing and do not like being stopped.

This can be challenging for parents and signals that it may be time to begin employing 'discipline'.

The Purpose of Discipline

Parents often ask childcare professionals for advice on how to employ discipline that is not only effective, but also positive. But, you may wonder, isn't the term 'positive discipline' a contradiction?

How can it be possible to discipline a child in a positive way? After all, isn't discipline supposed to be a negative experience, designed to teach a child not to repeat an undesirable behaviour?

Perhaps in Dickensian England it was, but we live in slightly more enlightened times. In order to properly answer these questions, it is important first to ask a more basic question:

What is the real PURPOSE of discipline?

And, as is often the case when dealing with young children, in order to begin answering this question, it is helpful at the outset to consider *what it is not*.

The purpose of discipline is not simply to produce a compliant and obedient child.

Clearly, the most immediate purpose of discipline is to protect your child from danger. The toddler who repeatedly jumps on the couch next to a glass window, for example, requires a parent to communicate a clear message to avoid serious harm.

In social terms, however, the principle objective of discipline is to teach children what they must do in order to maintain good relations with other people.

This involves learning to regulate their behaviour to ensure it is socially acceptable. By setting rules, boundaries and limits, parents teach children the 'behavioural regulation' (more commonly referred to as 'self-control'), which they can subsequently apply at school and throughout their lives.

The way we discipline our children may well become the way they 'self-regulate' when they become an adult. The disciplinary commands or expectations of the parent often become the self-talk of the child. For this reason, a person's life quality can be significantly affected by the way the person has been disciplined in childhood.

It is vitally important, therefore, that parents do all they can to learn how to discipline their children in a positive way.

So, What *Is* Discipline?

The Oxford Dictionary includes a wide variety of definitions for discipline, including:

- *A branch of instruction or learning*
- *Mental and moral training*
- *Control or order maintained among schoolboys, soldiers, prisoners etc.*
- *A system of rules for conduct*
- *To bring under control by training in obedience*
- *Chastisement*

Of course, developing a disciplinary approach for a pre-schooler will involve elements of each of these definitions, but we are particularly interested in the notion of positive discipline – in how we might achieve these things in a way which allows our children to:

 i) Learn 'self-control'

 ii) Recognise limits and boundaries

 iii) Know what is acceptable and unacceptable behaviour in the wider society

 iv) Know when to stop

In this context, words such as 'control', 'chastisement', 'order' and 'obedience' carry unfortunate subtexts. If our ultimate goal is that our children develop 'intrinsic (self-)discipline', then terms such as 'modifying', 'teaching', 'guiding' and 'nurturing' behaviour sit more comfortably with the notion of 'positive discipline'.

Discipline is most often about employing a method to stop an undesirable behaviour and replace it with a more desirable one. As your child grows, discipline moves from the simple commands and instructions issued to toddlers to more complex requests made of children and teenagers.

As children are able to comprehend, discipline can guide them toward desirable behaviours such as ensuring they:

- Demonstrate consideration for others

- Maintain a consistent self-care routine

- Choose safe behaviour

- Follow family routines and manners

Ideally, positive discipline allows the child freedom to choose, but it is not an unbridled freedom. As Charles Kingsley put it almost 200 years ago:

There are two freedoms — the false, where a man is free to do what he likes; the true, where he is free to do what he ought.

Disciplining a child requires much thought and preparation. Parents need to be conscious about discipline, and be clear on their personal 'discipline policy'.

This involves asking themselves questions such as:

- *Exactly how am I going to discipline my child?*

- *What behaviour do I find acceptable, and what is unacceptable?*

- *What will my rules and punishments be?*

- *Do I believe in punishment?*

- *What disciplinary methods do I think are appropriate?*

and, most of all,

- *How do I discipline so that overall, it leads to a positive outcome?*

How Do I Discipline My Child in a Positive Way?

The answers to the questions above, and subsequently the way parents choose to discipline their children will depend largely on their values, culture and beliefs. Around the world, children are disciplined in many different ways. The research on the subject also acknowledges that there is no one right way to discipline. There are, however, some methods which are more successful than others in producing self-discipline, and some which, while they were once tolerated, are no longer acceptable.

For instance, spanking children was considered a reasonable means of applying discipline prior to approximately 1980. Sayings such as '*Spare the rod, spoil the child*' reinforced not only the acceptability of spanking but its necessity.

Current early childhood research almost unanimously discourages any form of corporal punishment for children, at any time. Fortunately there is a significant amount of guidance available to parents offering alternative strategies which are not only effective, but also positive.

Modern discipline starts with being prepared, and setting ground rules in the belief that this will minimise the need for high emotional discipline.

Positive Preparation

Here are some suggestions to follow in that preparation.

1. Put Valuables Out of Reach

A common cause of tension for parents arises when their toddler learns to reach items of value on bookshelves and in cabinets. Many a parent has dashed across the room just in time to save Grandma's antique china from the eager clutches of a toddler.

Young children do not understand value in a monetary sense, and they also do not understand that certain items are more easily broken than others. They just think everything is there to be investigated. They aren't being bad, and they won't really understand why you might become upset when they pick up one item as opposed to another.

Acknowledging this reality, parents can avoid on-going stress by removing valuable objects from within their toddler's reach. Such objects can be placed on higher shelves or stored away temporarily. Our homes may look somewhat bare for a period of time, but at least they will be peaceful and intact!

Once a child has reached about four or five years of age, it is reasonable to create a rule that some items — or even rooms — in the house are 'out of bounds' and that there will be consequences if this rule is broken.

2. Set 'Positively Stated' Rules

Children need to know what the rules are, so they have the opportunity to follow them.

Consider your child's age when making the rules, because they need to be fair and reasonable. A toddler may not be capable of following the rule '*Clean up when you're finished playing*', yet a four- or five-year-old is. A toddler may be more able to follow a rule like '*Be gentle with doggie*'.

More repetition is required when setting rules for toddlers, such as acting out physically the desired behaviour. For example, parents can physically demonstrate being gentle by patting the dog gently, and repeating the phrase 'be gentle' in connection with the action.

As discussed earlier in this chapter, we should tell our children what we want them to do, not what we don't want them to do.

This means we need to state rules in the positive, where the child is moving 'towards' a desirable behaviour rather than 'away from' an undesirable one. Examples of 'positively stated' rules for a four-year-old are:

- Always walk when you are in the living-room
(rather than '*Don't run in the living-room*')

- Put your shoes in the wardrobe
(rather than '*Don't leave your shoes lying around*')

- Clean up when you've finished playing
(rather than '*Don't leave toys all over the house*')

- Take your plate to the sink when you've finished dinner
(rather than '*Don't leave your plate at the table after dinner*')

Children love being involved in rule making, and by the time they are four or five years of age they are capable of doing so. Together you could make a poster of the rules, using simple words and matching pictures, demonstrating the desired behaviour.

Even photographing your children actually doing the desired behaviour — that is, cleaning up or taking their plate to the sink — and putting the photos on the poster can be extremely effective.

Consequences for breaking rules can even be overtly stated. It may be worthwhile to ask your children what they think is an appropriate consequence if a rule is broken. Ask using a question like *'What do you think should happen if you break this rule?'* and give them some time to consider some options.

Sometimes, children can be far harsher than parents, so some discussion and gentle guidance is necessary.

3. Create Routines

Like rules, routines communicate very clear expectations to young children. They know what to do at different times of the day, such as getting ready for pre-school in the morning or preparing for bed at night.

When these expectations are clear and set, it means there is no need for continuous negotiation whenever the situation arises.

Childcare centres operate according to daily routines because they know the comfort and calm it produces in children. Routines are also empowering for children, because they are able to predict parts of their life which gives a sense of control over it.

Routines can be created by parents and children together. Like rules, when children have been involved in their creation they are more likely to follow them.

4. Model Desirable Behaviour

One of the most popular videos of recent years on *America's Funniest Home Videos* shows a boy of about four, holding a toy golf club. When the mother, who is taking the video, asks him to play golf *'just like Daddy'*, the boy lines up the ball, takes an elegant swing, and watches the ball disappear off-screen. He waits for about two seconds, then slams the club onto the floor shouting 'DAMMIT!' at the top of his voice.

Out of the mouths of babes...

Children love to imitate adults, especially their parents. As they do not discriminate between good and bad behaviour, they will copy everything they see and hear, often to the embarrassment of parents! This is why it is important for parents to model desired behaviours for their children.

Children learn more from what you actually do than from what you tell them to do, which is why it's all the more important to set a good example.

If you want your children to take their plate to the kitchen after dinner, you must do it. If you want them to put their shoes away in the wardrobe, then so must you. And if you ask them to clean up after playing, you should also clean up after yourself as well.

It's only fair to apply to yourself the same rules that you lay down for your children.

We will discuss modelling in more detail soon.

5. Pay Attention to Desirable Behaviour

When your child has displayed a desirable behaviour unprompted, it is good to pay attention to that behaviour. Acknowledging the behaviour by making a comment such as '*I see you've cleaned up your toys. You are so good at cleaning up now!*' reinforces the behaviour in a very powerful way.

Often children receive more attention when they display negative behaviours because the parent has to spend time focussing on the child to correct the behaviour.

Some areas of early childhood theory caution that the attention a child receives during discipline can reinforce negative behaviour. This is because children crave and love attention, and are quite prepared to behave negatively if they know that's how they will get it.

By consciously choosing to look out for your child's positive behaviours and giving him/her attention when you notice them, you are encouraging him/her to repeat that behaviour.

6. Give Choices Where Possible

To a young child intent on expressing newfound individuality, it can be very frustrating to follow rules and do as others say.

Children long for opportunities where they can make a choice about something. Parents can easily provide these opportunities by allowing them to make choices on issues such as:

- Clothing — 'Blue jeans or red?'
- Food — 'Apple or banana?'
- Bedtime stories — 'Little Red Riding Hood or Cinderella?'

While you, as parents, still have some degree of control — your children are still wearing jeans, eating healthy fruit and reading — they have also been empowered to make a decision which affects their life.

7. Imagine the World from Your Pre-schooler's Point of View

Toddlers and pre-schoolers are different from adults.

As we have seen earlier, they have shorter attention spans and memories, and even if you've set them a rule they can simply forget it.

They can only follow one instruction at a time, have limited language ability and have far less experience of the world.

They can also become very absorbed in what they are doing and can shut out the rest of their environment to focus on the enquiry at hand, which means they seem to ignore when someone is speaking to them.

When giving an instruction to your child, always ask yourself:

- Did my child hear me, or was s/he too involved in what s/he was doing?
- Did my child understand what I said?
- Was I speaking clearly and using language s/he can understand?

Because they can be so absorbed in what they are doing, children also need some warning before they are expected to finish an activity. We all know what it is like to be so absorbed in something that we want to keep doing it, even when someone else is demanding our attention.

It is reasonable for parents to give their child a warning of a few minutes before they are to stop an activity. Using a phrase such as 'Five minutes till pack-up time', or 'You need to finish what you are doing in five minutes so we can go' is enough to prompt a child to begin wrapping up.

Young children may not know exactly how long five minutes is, but they will at least register that they will need to finish their activity in a short time span.

8. Parents United

Because parents may have had such different upbringings, they may also have very different ideas about how their own children should be disciplined. One partner may have experienced very liberal parenting, and the other partner may have had an extremely strict and regimented upbringing.

This is why parents need to discuss their discipline styles together and arrive at a style they are both happy to implement with their own children. Once done, they both need to commit to consistency with the approach and to supporting each other in presenting a 'united front' to their children.

As children get older, they become very adept at playing one parent off against the other. They know which parent will say 'yes' to a particular request. When parents are united and consistent in their discipline style, the boundaries are clear, making way for a more secure and harmonious home environment.

9. Sleep, Food and Bonding

As we have discussed in relation to Maslow's Needs, when children's basic physiological and belonging needs are met, they are able to operate at a much higher level, and this also means that their behaviour also improves.

Children misbehave and become emotionally fragile when they are tired and hungry. The first questions parents should ask themselves when they notice their child's behaviour deteriorating are:

- *Is she hungry?*
- *Is he tired?*

Children also need physical affection. Touch sets off calming physiological reactions in the body and brain.

Calm and emotionally secure children, who have plenty of bonding experiences with their parents, are less likely to misbehave. Hugging your child is perhaps one of the best ways to avoid the need to discipline.

10. Teach Them How to Do Things

Pre-schoolers are so intelligent and capable that it is easy to forget that there are still many things they do not know how to do.

Sometimes they may not follow a parent's request because they don't know how to do a particular thing. They need to be taught to do just about everything, from putting their toys away, getting dressed and making their beds, to patting the cat.

Take the time to teach your children how to do these basic tasks, understanding that you will need to show them quite a few times before they can do them independently. When you are sure they are competent at a given task, then it is okay to instruct them to do it when necessary.

Positive Discipline Strategies

While the preparatory measures described earlier are designed to minimise the need to discipline children, there will still be countless occasions when parents will need to use disciplinary strategies with their children.

Here are some widely accepted strategies that early childhood professionals advocate when disciplining pre-schoolers.

1. Ensure Your Child Has Heard You

As discussed, young children can become extremely absorbed in what they are doing. Whether painting a wall or squeezing the cat, they appear to operate in a world of their own at times, and seem to temporarily lose their sense of hearing. Oftentimes, it's not that they are ignoring or disobeying you, it's just that they genuinely cannot hear you.

When parents wish to stop their child on something, they need to ensure their child can hear their instructions.

Kneeling down so that you are facing your children at eye level is sure to capture their attention. Asking whether your child can hear you — 'Can you hear Mummy talking to you?' and then giving the instruction you wish to give him/her, for example 'Be gentle with the cat', is a very effective strategy.

2. Distraction

As mentioned earlier, because of their immature memories and attention spans, distraction works well for babies and younger toddlers.

It's simply a matter of picking them up and moving them away from what they are doing, and drawing their attention to something else. As they understand more language, it is perfectly okay to accompany their removal with a simple instruction, such as 'Away from the china', followed by a comment relating to what you are distracting them with, such as 'Here's your big drum'.

This strategy is less effective once they are about 18 months to two years old.

3. Re-direction

Sometimes young children discover a new activity and delight in practising it.

Often, there isn't a problem with what they are doing — it's how they are doing it and what they are using to do it. When this happens, re-direction is required.

For example, if your toddler has discovered the delights of throwing a 'ball', it may use anything in its environment to throw — books, toys, or grandma's china — as if everything is a ball!

In this circumstance, rather than becoming angry, try offering your child a ball, saying something like '*We throw balls. We must only put our toys down gently*'.

Likewise, if your children are drawing on the walls (because they believe anything clean is a canvas!), offer them some paper.

Rather than reprimanding your children, take a moment to consider the world from their point of view, understanding that they haven't quite developed the discernment which enables them to differentiate one item or concept from another.

4. Time Out

Time out is a widely accepted disciplinary strategy.

It works in a number of ways, firstly because removing the children from the situation immediately stops the undesirable behaviour. They are then given an opportunity to reflect on their behaviour.

Time out also diffuses a potentially heightened emotional situation, allowing everyone to calm down.

It is important to establish a suitable time-out place in your home, free of distractions. Time out should always be in the same place, so that the child is anchored to that one spot and associates time out with one area.

Some families choose a corner of the living room, the laundry or perhaps a spot in the hallway. Bedrooms are not usually suitable places for time out because children can easily become distracted by toys and be having such a fun time that they forget about reflecting on their behaviour.

A chair or mat is often placed in the time-out area so that the child can sit comfortably.

It is generally recommended that the length of time a child stays in time out be one minute per year of age. Parents can even use a kitchen timer to ensure the time is accurate and avoid situations where they become distracted and forget their child is in there!

Children can even watch the timer, knowing they are there for a limited time. Young children have shorter memories, and if they are in time out for too long they will forget why they were put there in the first place.

Once the children have been in time out for the set length of time, parents need to explain to their children again why they had to go to time out.

This involves talking about what happened, why their behaviour was unacceptable and what they need to be doing in the future.

For instance, a parent might say:

You had to go to time out because you hit your friend. Hitting is wrong. If you are angry, what is a better thing to do, instead of hitting? Do you think it might be better to walk away, or talk to an adult who can help you? We should always be gentle with our friends, shouldn't we?

Giving children a hug at this point reassures them that your love for them is still there even though they have made a mistake.

5. Natural and 'Apposite' Consequences

Discipline instils a sense of 'cause and effect', or consequence, into a young person's growing knowledge of right and wrong.

Through experiencing these consequences children learn, *if I do this, then that will happen*, because they understand that there is a link between their behaviour and an outcome.

As adults, consequences occur in our lives which are often a natural result of a decision we have made. For instance, if we choose to speed on a rainy day and have a car accident, we understand that our behaviour has led to a natural consequence. We learn from this mistake.

Children also experience natural consequences. For instance if a child throws a toy and breaks it, the natural consequence will be that s/he will no longer be able to play with that toy.

The child will also learn that it is wrong — or at least, inconvenient — to break things.

Whenever a natural consequence occurs, it is helpful for parents to discuss the event with their children and then reinforce an alternative positive behaviour in the future with phrases, such as '*It's better to always be gentle with your toys*'.

Like 'natural' consequences, 'apposite' consequences are also linked to the negative behaviour. The word *apposite* means 'fitting' or 'appropriate', and apposite consequences differ from natural consequences, in that they are imposed by a parent or someone else in authority — that is, although they follow from the action, they are not necessarily an automatic 'natural' consequence.

For example, if a child bites his/her playgroup friend, a natural consequence could be the friend biting the child back, though this is a very undesirable outcome!

An apposite consequence, on the other hand, would be for the mother to remove the child from the play area for some time out, with a phrase such as 'Biting is wrong. You need some time out. You can only play if you are kind'.

When children have had some time out, the parent needs to give a directive which reminds them of the desired behaviour, such as 'Play gently with your friends', to instil expected behaviour. From this they will understand that it is wrong to cause harm to another person.

Consequences, whether natural or imposed, send a strong message that the immediately preceding behaviour is unacceptable.

6. Be Flexible

Flexibility is required when applying the disciplinary strategies, because:

    i) *A strategy that is successful at one time may not be successful at another.*

    ii) *Different children respond differently to different strategies.*

7. Guiding Behaviour with Questions

Discipline is undoubtedly about changing behaviour, but it is also about activating thinking in your child.

Consider that it is the change in thinking that will create the longer term changes in outward behaviour. One way parents can change thinking in their children is to learn the art of asking questions which activate 'fertile thinking'.

Parents often use questions when asserting discipline. However, we must understand that some questions are better than others.

Take a situation where your child has left his/her shoes in the hallway after being told many times in the past to put them away in the cupboard.

As we know, young children have developing memories and need regular reminding of the rules before they can independently follow them.

In this situation, a parent may typically give a simple direction, such as 'Put your shoes away now, please', which works because it is clear and unambiguous, not to mention polite with a 'please' added.

When time is short and you just need to get the job done, a direct instruction is very effective.

Emotive questions such as *'How many times have I told you? Don't you think I'm getting sick and tired of telling you?'* provoke an emotional response, and though the child may put the shoes away, it is with reluctance — and the long-term lesson may very well not penetrate.

Fertile questions expect — and encourage — a response and, phrased correctly, serve to reinforce the reason behind the request.

'Sally, where do your shoes belong?', or *'Tim, where's a better place to put your shoes than in the hallway?'* requires your child to think of the appropriate response, such as *'In my shoe cupboard!'*.

This gives an opportunity for the parent to say *'That's right, good thinking. Off you go then and put them there. Next time pop your shoes there as soon as you take them off'* — which is a more positive interaction.

Of course, we do need to understand that even though you have asked a fertile question, your child may still need reminders multiple times more before the desired behaviour becomes a habit.

The objective here is to ask a question that will evoke an answer which makes the desirable behaviour *your child's idea*. We are always more committed to our own ideas.

By contrast if a parent asks a question like *'What are your shoes doing in the hallway again?'*, the natural unthinking response will be something like *'I just left them there. I forgot'*, which leads the child to set about creating excuses for the undesirable behaviour.

Asking questions for disciplinary purposes should always be about leading children to think of the desirable behaviour as if it's their idea, giving them the opportunity to be praised, thus reinforcing the behaviour.

What saves a man is to take a step.
Then another step.

Antoine de Saint-Exupery

CONCLUSION

Where to from Here?

Nineteenth Century Scottish author and reformer Samuel Smiles, once wrote:

Great results cannot be achieved at once; and we must be satisfied to advance in life as we walk, step by step.

In this book, we have taken our first important steps — examining some of the key 'needs' of your pre-schoolers, and strategies for addressing them.

In Volume Two, we will examine the art of Preparing Your Pre-School Children for Lifelong Learning, through:

Immersive Literacy — the Magic of Storytelling:
- Fun versus Phonics — The Difference between Reading and Decoding
- Narrative Intelligence — Why We Need to Develop It
- The Art of Prediction — Applying Creative Thinking to Shared Reading and Storytelling
- Using Story Time to Inspire Emotional Intelligence in Pre-Readers
- Enhancing Storytelling through Stimulating the Senses

Parenting for Creativity, an approach designed for:

- Encouraging Creativity in Your Child — How Creative Children Become Creative Adults
- Harnessing the Creative Power of Role-Play — Using Role-Play to Rehearse Life
- Promoting Everyday Creativity at Home — Ideas to Develop Creativity and Divergent Thinking Skills
- Asking Better Questions for Better Thinking — How to Make a Difference by Asking Great Questions When Your Children are Young

School Readiness, looking at:

- Different Approaches to Pre-Schooling
- Home Environment — Creating a Home in Which Your Pre-schooler Can Learn
- Some World Standards for School Readiness
- Making a Difference — Activities for Developing School Readiness at Home

And, saving the best to last:

A range of Playful Learning Activities that prove (in the words of Kathy Hirsh-Pasek and Roberta Michnick Golinkoff) — 'Play is Not a Four-Letter Word...'.

This important chapter will demonstrate that:

- Newborns Can Play Too — Outlining Activities for the First Few Months
- Learning to Play is Playing to Learn — Introducing Activities for Toddlers and Growing Pre-schoolers
- It is Great to Feel the Sun on Your Skin, the Wind in Your Hair — With Ideas for Proven Outdoor Activities

Our role as parents is to help our children move from their first faltering syllables to a constant conversation with the Universe. The journey from one to the other is one of adventure and discovery — and not to be missed. It is our privilege to walk the early miles together with them, as both guide and companion.

How well we guide them will play a significant part in determining the quality of that lifelong conversation — and the nature of the stories they will tell to their children.

We look forward to sharing a small part of that journey with you in the second, and concluding, volume of *Pre-school Parenting Secrets: Talking with the Sky*.

☙

Bibliography

For parents, carers or teachers who wish to read further on any of the topics in this book, we have included a list of books, articles and websites which may be of interest. The bibliography is organised by chapters, for easy reference.

Chapter One

Bowlby, J. (1969). Attachment and Loss: Vol.1, Attachment. New York: Basic Books.

Bowlby, J. (1982). Attachment. New York: Basic Books.

Bowlby, J. (1988). A Secure Base: Parent-child attachment and healthy human development. New York: Basic Books.

Comer, J.P. (1980). School Power. New York: The Free Press. Updated in 1992.

Fahlberg, V. (1988). Fitting the Pieces Together. London: British Agencies for Adoption and Fostering.

Field, T. (1995). Massage Therapy for Infants and Children. Dev. Behav. Pediatr. 16: 105–111.

Hirsh-Pasek, K. & R.M. Golinkoff (2003). Einstein Never Used Flashcards. New York: Rodale.

Hirsh-Pasek, K., R.M. Golinkoff, L.E.Berk & D.G.Singer (2009). A Mandate for Playful Learning in Preschool – Presenting the Evidence. New York: Oxford.

Maslow, A. (1943). 'A Theory of Human Motivation.' Originally Published in Psychological Review, 50, 370–396.

Maslow, A. (1954). Motivation and Personality. New York: Harper.

Chapter Two

Berk, Lee & Stanley Tan (1996). The Laughter-Immune Connection: from the American Association of Therapeutic Humor. www.aath.org Nov 1997.

Centre for Community Child Health (2007). Child behaviour: Overview of the literature. Monograph 3 in A.O'Hanlon, A. Patterson & J. Parham (Series Eds.), Promotion, Prevention and Early Intervention for Mental Health in General Practice. Adelaide: Australian Network for Promotion, Prevention and Early Intervention for Mental Health (Auseinet).

Cohen, J. George (1999). American Academy of Pediatrics Guide to Your Child's Sleep. New York: Villard.

Doidge, N. (2007). The Brain That Changes Itself.USA: Viking Penguin.

Fry Jr., W.F. (1992). The physiologic effects of humor, mirth, and laughter. JAMA, 267, 1857–1858.

Fry, W. (1977). The respiratory components of mirthful laughter. Journal of Biological Psychology, 19(2), 39–50.

Fuhr, J.E. & K.H.Barclay (1998). The Importance of Appropriate Nutrition and Nutrition Education, Young Children, 53(1), 74–80.

Horobin, K. & L.Acredolo (1986). The role of attentiveness, mobility history, and separation of hiding sites on stage IV search behavior. Journal of Experimental ChildPsychology, 41, 114–127.

Jensen, E. (2000). Brain Based Learning: Revised Edition. California: Sage Publications.

Kalamis, C. (2001). Laugh Your Way to Health. Choice Magazine, March 2001. Sydney: UNSW Press.

Kermoian, R. & J.J. Campos (1988). Locomotor experience: A facilitator of spatial cognitive development. ChildDevelopment, 59, 908–917.

McGhee, P. (1979). Humor: Its origin and development. San Francisco: W.H. Freeman.

McGhee, P. (1989). Humor and children's development: A guide to practical applications. New York: Haworth Press.

National Sleep Foundation (2002). Sleep In America Poll. www.sleepfoundation.org.

Puder, C. (2003). The Healthful Effects of Laughter. The International Child and Youth Care Network. On-line Article: Issue 55. http://www.cyc-net.org/cyc-online/cycol-0803-humour.html.

Roberts, S, M.B. Heyman & L. Tracy (1999). Feeding Your Child for Lifelong Health: Birth Through Age Six. USA: Bantam Books.

Siegler, S. & M.W. Alibali (2005). Children's Thinking Fourth Edition. New Jersey: Prentice Hall.

Silberg, J. (2004). The Learning Power of Laughter. Beltsville, MD: Gryphon House.

Torrance, E.P. & T. Wu (1981). A comparative longitudinal study of the adult creative achievements of elementary school children identified as highly intelligent and as highly creative. Creative Child and Adult Quarterly, 6, 71–76.

Videon, T.M. & C.K. Manning (2003). Influences on adolescent eating patterns: The importance of family meals. J Adolesc Health. Vol 32,365–373.

Wansink et al. (2008). Consequences of Belonging to the "Clean Plate Club". Archives of Pediatrics and Adolescent Medicine,162(10), 994 DOI: 10.1001/archpedi.162.10.994.

Weissbluth, M. (2003). Healthy Sleep Habits, Happy Child. London: Random House Publishing Group.

http://www.who.int/dietphysicalactivity/publications/facts/obesity/en/.

Wolf, J. (2008). A Bedtime Routine That Works: Creating A Routine That Helps Your Child Fall Asleep. www.singleparents.about.com/od/parenting/qt/bedtimeroutine.htm.

Yoo, SS., P.T.Hu, N.Gujar, F.A.Jolesz, M.P.Walker (2007). A deficit in the ability to form new human memories without sleep. Nature Neuroscienc. Vol 10: 385-392. http://www.nature.com/neuro/journal/v10/n3/abs/nn1851.html.

Chapter Three

Bernard, M.E. (1997). You can do it! How to boost your child's achievement in school. New York: Warner Books, pp. 336.

Bernard, M.E. (2003). Developing the social-emotional-motivational competence of young people with achievement and behavior problems: A guide for working with teachers and parents. Oakleigh, VIC: Australian Scholarships Group.

Bernard, M.E. (2004). Emotional resilience in children: Implications for Rational Emotive Education. Romanian Journal of Cognitive and Behavioral Psychotherapies, 4, pp 39–52.

Caselman, T. (2004). Impulse control: stop and think. Champaign, Il.: Research Press.

Coleman, D. (1991). 'A Bias Puts Self at the Center of Everything.' Psychological Updates: Articles on Psychology from The New York Times. Harper Collins Publishers, pp. 51–52.

Covey, S. (1989). The 7 Habits of Highly Effective People. New York: Simon & Schuster.

Epley, N., K. Carey, C. K. Morewedge & B. Keysar (2004). 'Perspective taking in children and adults: Equivalent egocentrism but differential correction.' Journal of Experimental Social Psychology. 40, 760–768.

Goldstein, S. & R. Brooks (2001). Raising Resilient Children. New York: Contemporary Books.

Goleman, D. (1995). Emotional intelligence: Why it can matter more than IQ. London: Bloomsbury Publishing Plc.

Grinder, J. & J. DeLozier (1987). Turtles All the Way Down: Prerequisites to Personal Genius. Scotts Valley, CA: Grinder & Associates.

Henderson, N., N. Sharp-Light, and Bonnie Benard (eds.). (1999). "Fostering Resiliency in Children and Youth: Four Basic Steps for Families, Educators, and Other Caring Adults," in Resiliency In Action: Practical Ideas for Overcoming Risks and Building Strengths in Youth, Families, and Communities, by San Diego, CA:Resiliency In Action, Inc. www.resiliency.com.

Piaget, J. & B. Inhelder (1948/1956). The Child's Conception of Space. London: Routledge and Paul Kegan.

Reivich, K. & A. Shatté (2002). The Resilience Factor. New York: Broadway Books.

Seligman, M.E.P. (1991). Learned Optimism. New York: Pocket Books.

Seligman, M.E.P. (1995). The Optimistic Child: A Revolutionary Approach to Raising Resilient Children. Sydney, NSW: Random House Australia.

Seligman, M. E. P., K. Reivich, L. Jaycox & J. Gillham (1995). The Optimistic Child. New York: Harper Perennial.

Seligman, M.E.P. (2002). Authentic Happiness: Using the new positive psychology to realise your potential for lasting fulfilment. New York: The Free Press.

Shoda, Y., W. Mischel & P. K. Peake (1990). Predicting adolescent cognitive and self-regulatory competencies from preschool delay of gratification: Identifying diagnostic conditions. Developmental Psychology, 26(6), 978–986.

Werner, E. & R.S. Smith (1992). Overcoming the Odds: High Risk Children from Birth to Adulthood. New York: Cornell University Press.

Chapter Four

Becker, H. (1952). "Social class variations in the teacher-pupil relationship." Journal of Educational Sociology, 25, 451–466.

Beedell, C. (1970). Residential life with children. London: Routledge.

Fox, R. & M. Krueger (1987). 'Social skills training: implications for child and youth care practice.' Journal of Child Care, 3(1), 1–7.

Gralinski, J.H., & C.B. Kopp (1993). Everyday rules for behaviour: Mothers' requests to young children. Developmental Psychology, 29, 573–584.

Hoghughi, M. (1988). Treating problem children: issues, methods and practice. London: Sage Publications.

Michigan Department of Education (2001). What Research says about Parent Involvement in Children's Education in Relation to Academic Achievement. State of Michigan.

Oesterreich, L. (2001). Understanding Children: Disciplining your Preschooler. Iowa State University. www.extension.iastate.edu/store.

Peine, H. A. & R. Howarth (1975,1993). Children and Parents: Everyday Problems of Behaviour. Utah: Two Goats Publishing.

Pringle, M. K. (1975). The Needs of Children. London: Hutchinson.

Rosenthal, R. & L. Jacobson (1968). Pygmalion in the Classroom. New York: Rinehart and Winston.

Shonkoff, J. & D. Phillips (2000). From Neurons To Neighbourhoods: The Science of Early Childhood Development. Washington D.C.: National Academy Press.

Skinner R.A. & J.P. Piek (2001). Psychosocial implications of poor motor co-ordination in children and adolescents. Human Movement Science, 20(12), 73–94.

Snyder, A. (2002). What makes a champion? Camberwell Vic: Penguin.

Ulrich, B.D. (1987). Perceptions of physical competence, motor competence and participation in organized sport: Their interrelationships in young children, Research Quarterly for Exercise and Sport, 58, 57–67.

Further Resources

http://smhp.psych.ucla.edu/qf/impulse.htm.

Coleman, D. (1991). 'A Bias Puts Self at the Center of Everything.' Psychological Updates: Articles on Psychology from The New York Times. Harper Collins Publishers, pp. 51–52.

Epley, N., K. Carey, C. K. Morewedge & B. Keysar (2004). 'Perspective taking in children and adults: Equivalent egocentrism but differential correction.' Journal of Experimental Social Psychology. 40, pp 760–768.

Gordon, Mary. http://www.theparentreport.com/resources/topics/family_life/teen/222.html.

http://www.indiaparenting.com/articles/data/art09_012.shtml.

Endnotes

1   Hirsh-Pasek, K., R.M. Golinkoff, L.E. Berk & D.G. Singer (2009). A Mandate for Playful Learning in Preschool – Presenting the Evidence. New York: Oxford.

Hirsh-Pasek, K., B. Pasek & R.M. Golinkoff (2009, September 21). Essay in: Sifting your Harvard questions, looking for parenting (and other) lessons. New York Times. http://thechoice.blogs.nytimes.com/2009/09/21/harvardquestions/#more-8381.

2   (i) Bowlby, J. (1969). Attachment and Loss: Vol.1, Attachment. New York: Basic Books.

        (ii) Bowlby, J. (1982). Attachment. New York: Basic Books.

        (iii) Bowlby, J. (1988). A Secure Base: Parent-child attachment and healthy human development. New York: Basic Books.

3   Fahlberg, V. (1988). Fitting the Pieces Together. London: British Agencies for Adoption and Fostering,

4   Field, T. (1995). Massage Therapy for Infants and Children. Dev. Behav. Pediatr, 16,105–111.

5   Bowlby, J. (1988). A Secure Base: Parent-child attachment and healthy human development. New York: Basic Books.

6   Maslow, A. (1943). 'A Theory of Human Motivation.' Originally Published in Psychological Review, 50, 370–396.

7   Comer, J.P. (1980). School Power. New York: The Free Press. Updated in 1992.

8   National Sleep Foundation (2002). Sleep In America Poll. www.sleepfoundation. org.

9   Centre for Community Child Health (2007). Child behaviour: Overview of the literature. Monograph 3 in A.O'Hanlon, A. Patterson & J. Parham (Series Eds.), Promotion, Prevention and Early Intervention for Mental Health in General Practice. Adelaide: Australian Network for Promotion, Prevention and Early Intervention for Mental Health (Auseinet).

10   Weissbluth, M. (2003). Healthy Sleep Habits, Happy Child. London: Random House Publishing Group.

11   Yoo, SS., P.T. Hu, N. Gujar, F.A. Jolesz, M.P. Walker (2007). A deficit in the ability to form new human memories without sleep. Nature Neuroscienc. Vol 10: 385–392. http://www.nature.com/neuro/journal/v10/n3/abs/nn1851.html.

12   Cohen, George J. (Ed.). (1999). American Academy of Pediatrics Guide to Your Child's Sleep. New York: Villard.

13   Wolf, J. (2008). A Bedtime Routine That Works: Creating A Routine That Helps Your Child Fall Asleep. www.singleparents.about.com/od/parenting/qt/bedtimeroutine. htm.

14   http://www.who.int/dietphysicalactivity/publications/facts/obesity/en/.

15   Pyramid Servings Intakes by US Children and Adults (1994–1996, 1998). US Department of Agriculture. Agricultural Research Service. Beltsville, MD, October 2000. Available at http://www.barc.usda.gov/bhnrc/cnrg.

16   Videon, T.M. & C.K. Manning (2003). Influences on adolescent eating patterns: The importance of family meals. J Adolesc Health. Vol 32:365–373.

17   Wansink et al. (2008). Consequences of Belonging to the "Clean Plate Club". Archives of Pediatrics and Adolescent Medicine,162(10): 994 DOI: 10.1001/ archpedi.162.10.994.

18   Roberts, S, M.B. Heyman & L. Tracy (1999). Feeding Your Child for Lifelong Health: Birth Through Age Six. USA: Bantam Books.

19   Fuhr, J.E. & K.H. Barclay (1998). The Importance of Appropriate Nutrition and Nutrition Education, Young Children, 53(1),74–80.

20   Find child-friendly recipes at:
      http://www.kids-cooking-activities.com/non-reader-recipes.html.
      http://www.wholefamily.com/aboutyourkids/child/recipes2.html.

21   Silberg, J. (2004). The Learning Power of Laughter. Beltsville, MD: Gryphon House.

22   Ibid.

23   Kalamis, C. (2001). Laugh Your Way to Health. Choice Magazine, March 2001. Sydney: UNSW Press.

24   Berk, Lee & Stanley Tan (1996). The Laughter-Immune Connection: from the American Association of Therapeutic Humor. www.aath.org, Nov 1997.

25   (i) Fry Jr., W.F. (1992). The physiologic effects of humor, mirth, and laughter. JAMA, 267,1857–1858.

      (ii) Berk, Lee & Stanley Tan (1996). Op cit.

26   Torrance, E. P. & T. Wu (1981). A comparative longitudinal study of the adult creative achievements of elementary school children identified as highly intelligent and as highly creative. Creative Child and Adult Quarterly, 6, 71–76.

27   Puder, C. (2003). The Healthful Effects of Laughter. The International Child and Youth Care Network. On-line Article: Issue 55. http://www.cyc-net.org/cyc-online/cycol-0803-humour.html.

28   McGhee, P. (1979). Humor: Its origin and development. San Francisco: W.H. Freeman.

      McGhee, P. (1989). Humor and children's development: A guide to practical applications. New York: Haworth Press.

29   Silberg, J. (2004). Op cit.

30   www.who.int – the World Health Organisation website.

31   Jensen, E. (2000). Brain Based Learning: Revised Edition. California: Sage Publications.

32   Ibid.

33   Doidge, N. (2007). The Brain That Changes Itself. USA: Viking Penguin.

34   (i) Horobin, K. & L. Acredolo (1986). The role of attentiveness, mobility history, and separation of hiding sites on stage IV search behavior. Journal of Experimental ChildPsychology, 41, 114–127.

      (ii) Kermoian, R. & J.J. Campos (1988). Locomotor experience: A facilitator of spatial cognitive development. Child Development, 59, 908–917.

35   http://www.darksideoftanning.com.au.

36   Reivich, K. & A. Shatté (2002). The Resilience Factor. New York: Broadway Books.

37   Seligman, M. E. P., K. Reivich, L. Jaycox & J. Gillham (1995). The Optimistic Child. New York: Harper Perennial.

38   Reivich, K. & A. Shatté (2002). Op cit.

39   Seligman, M. E. P. et. al. (1995). Op cit.

40   Goldstein, S. & R. Brooks (2001). Raising Resilient Children – Contemporary Books, New York.

41   Werner, E. & R.S. Smith (1992). Overcoming the Odds: High Risk Children from Birth to Adulthood – New York: Cornell University Press, pg 205.

42   Shoda, Y., W. Mischel & P.K. Peake (1990). Predicting adolescent cognitive and self-regulatory competencies from preschool delay of gratification: Identifying diagnostic conditions. Developmental Psychology, 26(6), 978–986.

43   Piaget, J. & B. Inhelder (1948/1956). The Child's Conception of Space. London: Routledge and Paul Kegan.

44   Epley, N., K. Carey, C.K. Morewedge & B. Keysar (2004). 'Perspective taking in children and adults: Equivalent egocentrism but differential correction.' Journal of Experimental Social Psychology, 40, 760–768.

45   Goleman, D. (1995). Emotional intelligence: Why it can matter more than IQ. London: Bloomsbury Publishing Plc.

46   Grinder, J. & J. DeLozier (1987). Turtles All the Way Down: Prerequisites to Personal Genius. Scotts Valley, CA: Grinder & Associates.

47   Ulrich, B.D. (1987). Perceptions of physical competence, motor competence and participation in organized sport: Their interrelationships in young children, Research Quarterly for Exercise and Sport, 58, 57–67.

48   From http://www.indiaparenting.com/articles/data/art09_012.shtml.

49   Skinner, R.A. & J.P. Piek (2001). Psychosocial implications of poor motor co-ordination in children and adolescents. Human Movement Science, 20(12), 73–94.

50   Snyder, A. (2002). What Makes a Champion? Camberwell Vic: Penguin, p 4.

51   See: http://www.tagnet.org/powerlines/OvMother.htm.

52   Caswell, B. & D. Chiem (2009). The Art of Communicating with your Child. Harper Collins Editions, Singapore.